Scots Wha Hae Tae!

WHA'S LIKE US?
DAMN FEW AND
THEY'RE A' DEID!

Alasdair Anderson
Douglas McNaughton
Martin Coventry

GOBLINSHED
Musselburgh

Scots Wha Hae Tae!

First Published 2002
© Alasdair Anderson, Douglas McNaughton
and Martin Coventry 2002

Published by GOBLINSHEAD
130B Inveresk Road
Musselburgh EH21 7AY Scotland
tel 0131 665 2894; *fax* 0131 653 6566
email goblinshead@sol.co.uk

British Library Cataloguing in Publication Data
A catalogue record for this book is available from the
British Library.

ISBN 1 899874 41 0

Typeset by GOBLINSHEAD using Desktop Publishing

If you would like a colour catalogue of our
publications, please contact the publishers at
Goblinshead, 130B Inveresk Road,
Musselburgh EH21 7AY, Scotland, UK.

Also available
Scots Wha Hae!
The first instalment of the popular and amusing work.
1 899874 35 6 £5.95

Available from bookshops and other outlets or from the publisher
above (send a cheque for £5.95 (postage and packing is free) made
out to Goblinshead, with your name and address to Orders,
Goblinshead, 130B Inveresk Road, Musselburgh EH21 7AY).

Introduction

Welcome to a new and even fresher look at Scottish history. It's another romp through the country's past, with the usual linger on Mary, Queen of Scots and John Knox. This time we have managed to omit most of the 17th century.

As ever, this book cannot be recommended for exam revision, but many of the most unlikely articles are actually based on true events. Traditionally Kenneth III was killed with a machine loaded with poison, Cupar did turn down a clean water system, and government soldiers at Culloden did bedaub each other in Jacobite blood.

Many of the old favourites are back again, such as new definitions for Scottish place names, are you still Scottish (find out with our quiz), and some unique collectible bears. There are even some new items such as historic TV schedules, the tourist guide to Keicha, and the Braveheart Board Game.

We hope you enjoy reading this as much as we enjoyed writing it.

AA, DMcN and MC
Musselburgh, March 2002

Acknowledgements
Thanks to Jane Barbour for unearthing 'To a Prostate', Martin from Germany for the info about European attitudes to Scotland in the 18th century, and Joyce Miller for the photo of the John Knox Collectible Bear. Thanks also to everyone who made our first outpouring 'Scots Wha Hae!' so successful.

Emergency Scottish History

All the key facts and figures at your fingertips! Never be at a loss when friends start talking history down the pub. No more embarrassment when your mother-in-law alludes to John Knox. Impress your boss with a few salient dates! Pass a (very simple) exam! With this handy sheet you too can be at the centre of the social whirl and ready for anything.

10,000-5000 BC First people arrive. They live mainly on the coast.

4000 BC Skara Brae (a stone village), Maes Howe (a stone tomb) and Brodgar and Callanish (standing stones) confirm we're in the Stone Age.

2300-500 BC Beaker people living in the Bronze Age. (No not the Muppets!)

1000-400 BC Celtic people arrive. (Rangers came later.) It's the Iron Age now so people start using iron. They build hillforts and brochs, which look like cooling towers for power stations.

79-84 AD Romans! We set out to give them what for at Mons Graupius and lose, bugger!

120-208 But here's the proof we're not beaten. Romans have to build Hadrian's Wall to keep us out.

503-63 The Scots turn up from Ireland. They call their kingdom Dalriada, MacErc is king! He brings along a Stone of Destiny, well maybe. There's a special offer on converting to Christianity, marketing by St Columba.

685 Battle of Nechtansmere against the kingdom of Northumberland. A great victory for the Picts, spin on this King Ecgfrith!

843 Kenneth MacAlpin, a Scot, unites the kingdom and it's the last we hear from the Picts except for some fancy symbol stones. Now it's the turn of the Vikings to be unpleasant and do a spot of ravaging.

859-1057 A revolving door is installed in the palace and a parade of Constantines, Donalds and Malcolms all rapidly pass through. Macbeth (contrary to certain plays) rules quite ably for 17 years before dying in battle in 1057 against the forces of Malcolm Canmore.

1057-1286 St Margaret marries Malcolm (old Big Head). There is a waning of Celtic influence but a lot of new abbeys. A period of consolidation with just a hint of independence, buggered up by the death of Alexander III in 1286. This plunges us into a war with the English.

1296 Edward I invades and the first Battle of Dunbar (there's another one).

1297-1305 William Wallace (respect), our Braveheart, but meets an untidy end. Well, untidy if you're the cleaner as there is a lot of blood and intestines lying about afterwards.

1314-29 It's getting exciting now. Robert the Bruce wins the Battle of Bannockburn (1314). In the Declaration of Arbroath (1320) we write to the Pope, telling him we should be free and the English are nasty.

1329 Edward III recognises Scotland's independence, but it won't last.

1330-1423 Uneventful. We keep our hand in with some pointless fighting.

1424 James I. First in a long line of Stewart rulers, most called James, most dying violently.

1513 Catastrophe at Flodden. In a pointless war, James IV manages to snatch defeat from the jaws of victory against the English and gets slain.

1513-57 Fight, fight, fight: again with the English

1558-87 Mary, Queen of Scots. Rizzio murdered in 1565. Her estranged husband, Darnley, murdered in 1567. Mary, herself, after a long imprisonment by her cousin Elizabeth, effectively murdered in 1587. John Knox stokes up the fires of the Reformation.

1603-25 Just the one king in Britain now and he is Scottish! James VI. But let's face it, he was glad to be out of Scotland.

1625-49 National Covenant of 1638, then a civil war which culminates in the execution of Charles I. Beginning of the end for Stewarts as kings.

1650 Cromwell wins at Dunbar and invades Scotland.

1660-89 Charles II monarchy restored after Cromwell's administration. Then James VII, who very quickly becomes an ex-king (and head Jacobite) as he runs away to be replaced by William of Orange.

1689 Battle of Killiecrankie a victory for Jacobites but death of Bonnie Dundee (our very own Bloody Clavers!).

1692 Massacre of Glencoe: Campbells are beastly to MacDonalds

1698 Darien Scheme: half of the wealth in Scotland went down the pan, or Panama as the academics call it.

1707 Union of the parliaments of Scotland and England.

1715 Stewarts are at it again: James VIII tries to regain the throne but fails as Jacobite Rising fizzles out, like a long-opened bottle of Irn Bru.

1745-46 Had he learnt nothing from his old dad? Bonnie Prince Charlie has another go. He loses Culloden: the last pitched battle on British soil. Charlie retires to a life of philandering, while Highlands are punished.

1790 The Clearances. There is still a great deal of bitterness about this.

1800 We're on the home straight now with education, trade and culture replacing the traditional Scottish pastime of killing each other and the English: many Scots go abroad and kill foreign chaps.

1999 That's about it, unless you want to count the establishment of the Scottish Parliament.

Scots Wha Hae Tae!

Famous Scottish Songs

Scots Wha Hae

Scots weigh hay for faultless bread,
Tots warm prunes were often fed,
Welcome to your garden shed,
Or to pay TV!
Nose the hay, and nose the flower;
See the affronted cattle glower;
Ball cock fault floods Edward's shower
Blame the STD!

Who will be an Indian brave?
Cackling squaw is so deranged?
Laddie needs a toilet grave?
Let him turn and pee!
Wafer thin mints, slim and tall,
Three-ton bride kills mother-in-law,
Henman's hand or tennis ball,
Let him roll on me!

Buy a prison ball and chains!
Buy your sons four two-wheeled wains!
We will inject our deepest veins,
With crack and ecstasy!
Play the pipes you cry and bawl!
Tie racks fall to rabid crows!
Salad leaves in every bowl!
Lettuce do or beet!

Things to see in
Neolithic Scotland

Fancy a day out? Come to Neolithic Scotland. There's so much to see and do! It's really great!

Visit the latest showhouses at Skara Brae. There are model farms to inspect at Knap of Howar, Papa Westray and at Pettigarth's Field on Shetland. And go round the pottery factory. In the 'seconds' shop you can buy Stone Age pottery with its distinctive 'grooved ware' finish and elegant bucket shape.

Burial Cairns and Tombs

For a reflective day out you can inspect the 12-chamber tombs at Midhowe, Rousay in Orkney or the double-storey mausoleum at Taversoe Tuick, where the nobs are buried.

For something unusual, look at the triangular arrangement of stones on the Blackhammer mound on Rousay, or admire the Dwarfie Stane, Hoy, a rock-cut tomb with a passage and two chambers.

Standing Stones

Enjoy a charming local custom at the holed stone at Ballymeanoch, Kilmartin Glen, traditionally used for sealing contracts – the parties join hands through the hole in the stone: marriages a speciality!

Stone Circles

Visit the granite boulders of the Torhouse circle, Wigtown, or admire the slim pillars of gneiss which make up the famous lunar observatory at the Callanish circle on Lewis. If scale is your thing, try the ring of Brodgar on Orkney with its 60 stones, or the biggest circle in Scotland, the Twelve Apostles circle at Dumfries – the ideal settings for ceremonies, sacrifices and picnics.

It's not all stone circles though: you can see a horse-shoe-shaped arrangement of stones at Achavanich and a fan-shaped setting, the Hill o' Many Stanes, in Caithness.

Henges

If you're a hengespotter, Neolithic Scotland is the place for you! These circular earthworks are the wonders of the age. Who wouldn't enjoy a bank surrounding a ditch? Visit a henge today. Entry is into a central area via a causeway across the ditch and a passage through the bank.

Visit Balfarg Henge in Fife to see the unusual timber circle and stone circle, and go to Cairnpapple in West Lothian to see the 24 stones within the henge. The Stones of Stenness on Orkney mainland are a popular venue for ritual feasts and community gatherings, and pop festivals.

Ceremonial Avenues

If you like walking about ceremonially, why not try walking along a Scottish ceremonial avenue? These are formed of long ditches with the soil usually banked on the inner edge. Visit the Cleaven Dyke in Perthshire for a fine example, originally a burial mound and now extended to create a raised bank over two km long. Ideal for a country walk on a fine day.

Neolithic Scotland - It's Really Great!
Issued by The Neolithic Scotland Tourist Board

TV Guide

12.0   **Changing Tombs**
Laurence Llewelyn-Bowen visits Maes Howe and *frou-frous*
the place up a bit with some throw pillows, chiffon drapes,
and a fabulous candelabra made of driftwood.

12.30   **Ready, Steady, Cook**
Ainsley Harriett presides over another edition of the popular
cookery show. This week, Gordon Ramsay has to make
something of Team A's mystery ingredient, shellfish and
more shellfish, while Nick Nairn struggles with Team B's
surprise combination of shellfish and grass.

1.0   **News**
Kirsty Wark reports there is no news – yet.

1.01   **I Love Last Week**
The popular nostalgia show looks back at last week, when
living in caves was all the rage.

3.0   **I Love Yesterday Lunchtime**
Combined nostalgia and cookery programme.

4.0   **I Love Last Night's TV**
Combined nostalgia and TV review programme

4.15   **I Love Breakfast Time**
Combined nostalgia and early morning TV.

4.26   **Closedown**
We have run out of history to be nostalgic about. Normal
service will be resumed as soon as something happens.

Scottish Journeys

It's a long way to Lybster from Achavanich, but I'm a fit
man and I can easily make the journey in two hours. Och,
there are some of my neighbours who are talking about
using these new-fangled ponies. But I'm not sure I hold
with them. To be honest, if the gods had wanted us to get
on the back of a horse they'd have made our rear ends out
of granite. I can carry a basket of parsnips there, and bring
back some herring for the supper.

Callanish Stones Slammed

Local people on Lewis in the Western Isles have dubbed the new development at Callanish as 'an eyesore'. These arrangements of standing stones have been erected as the only accurate lunar observatory in the world. The main setting at Callanish consists of a cross-shaped of stones up to 20-feet tall. There are numerous other single monoliths, as well as smaller circles in the general vicinity.

'I cannot see what the fuss is about,' said local resident Angela Og. 'They may call this progress but frankly what is it good for? I mean when the moon is full you can see it, can't you?'

Environmentalists have also slammed the standing stones. 'This was an area of unrivalled natural beauty,' thundered Donald Og for the 'Friends of the Large Object on Which We Are Living Which May Be a Giant Porpoise, Whale, Turtle or Simply A Huge Ball of Rock and Metal Hurtling Through Space'. 'Now if these stones at Callanish did something useful, perhaps if it was a giant wind farm, which produced, well, something useful like a magical power which could run machinery, light and heat houses, and allow people to communicate over hundreds of miles. We can look forward to these things in the future, I guess. Complaining is timeless, though.'

Agri-cola: he's the real thing

Sparkling, full of life and packed with wholesome Roman goodness. Yes, Agri-cola wanted to teach the Scots to sing in perfect harmony.

In 80, he set up a marketing campaign that would take the message to the heart of this new territory. First he sent his crack sales managers in, with tight budgets and aggressive targets. They set up a number of branch offices in Perthshire and Aberdeenshire. The Roman CEO, Tacitus, was eager that they were up and in business as soon as possible.

The biggest challenge came when a rival conglomerate the Caledonii initiated a trade war. They finally had a heated exchange of memos and sharply worded letters in 84. Stung by some of the pointed criticism, especially that aimed at his personal development plans, the Scottish Director of Marketing, Calgacus, was too upset to continue and retired to spend more time with his family.

Although the battle had been won and new markets opened up, the Romans found that many of the potential customers weren't sold on Agri-cola and reluctantly had to accept there probably wouldn't be a forum on every street corner.

SCOTLAND INVADED

The Roman Empire began its conquest of Scotland yesterday as hordes of legionnaires crossed the border from England and marched north. The Romans have long sought to subjugate the Caledonians, but for the last few years they have stayed south of the border, restricting their campaign to attacks on isolated villages followed by retrenchment during the winter months.

However, under the command of Agricola, the legions are making a concerted effort to destroy as many hill forts as they can, and it seems certain that the Emperor Domitian has commanded a 'one-big-push' effort.

Defeat seems likely. Although the Scottish tribes have recently buried their differences and allied themselves together against the Romans, the playing field is far from level. With 26,000 highly trained and well-equipped troops from the greatest empire the world has ever seen, the Roman force vastly outguns the half-starved army being assembled by Calgacus.

But despite this, our spirit will not falter. We will take arms to protect our homeland, we will stand fast against the enemy, and we will defend Caledonia to the last drop of Scottish blood.

Scotland will prevail!

Ninth Roman Legion Lost in Paisley

The Ninth Roman Legion, while on vacation in Renfrewshire, nipped into the Volunteer Arms for some light refreshments, a packet of peanuts and to ask for directions to the bath-house at Bearsden. They have not been seen since.

Can you help?

Reports have been made of togas changing hands for two chickens in down-town Paisley, and a centurion's helmet was being used as a chamber pot in Clydebank.

What Did the Romans Ever Do For Us?

We spoke to some very angry Scots about the Romans. They were not happy about the effect that the Italian invaders had had on the infrastructure of Scotland.

'They never gave us anything. When you look at other countries – they got warm baths, toilet facilities, town planning, fancy villas, plumbing, decent roads, trade with the rest of Europe, a stable economy.'

'Some of them got an entertainment zone, you know – theatres, arenas and circuses, and decent bars as well. My brother-in-law slurred something about the beer being pretty good.'

'Look at those bloody great viaducts. We'd have liked one of them. But no! We got nothing!'

'All we got was that security wall to stop us joining in the fun.'

But you did spend all your time fighting them. You didn't exactly make them feel welcome, did you? Constantly killing people. Whipping off your clothes, painting your bottom blue, and jumping out of trees on top of them is a little anti-social, don't you think?

'I suppose so.'

If you'd wanted all of life's little luxuries, wouldn't it have been better just to have pretended to fight and then hoisted the white flag as soon as possible?

'What, like those effeminate flower arrangers in the south of Britain? Well, of course with hindsight ...'

'It was pretty obvious to me: you just had to take a look at Gaul or Britannia.'

'Alright, alright, we cocked it up. There's no need to rub it in. Why didn't they tell us about the benefits first? It just isn't fair.'

And there we must leave them ruing their lot.

Genuine Scottish Holy Relic
The Skull of St Ninian As A Baby
Limited Edition of only 500

St Ninian introduced Christianity to the general population of Scotland around 403 or so, after the withdrawal of the Roman legions from Britain. St Ninian was educated at Rome and founded a religious order at Whithorn, *Candida Casa*.

Now you can own a genuine relic of the Father of Scottish Christianity – with our exclusive, if somewhat disturbing, *The Skull of St Ninian As A Baby*.

Magnificently Detailed in Finest Quality Modelling Clay, Capturing for All Eternity the Dignity of St Ninian

> ### *The Skull of St Ninian*
> ### *As A Baby has so many uses:*
> - Paperweight
> - Bookend
> - Handy small missile to throw at your children
> - Hockey Ball
> - Thing to put in your washing machine full of washing liquid
> - Thermos flask

The Skull of St Ninian As A Baby comes complete with a handsome display stand, carved from a piece of finest Scottish firewood.

Accept No Imitations

ORDER FORM

I left school at 14 and worked in a jute mill/jam mill (delete as appropriate) for 50 years. I've never got the hang of this new money so I've no idea what I'm about to sign. And those twenty pences are so fiddly. I understand that any complaints I may have about the quality of the Skull of St Ninian As A Baby will be met with incredulity by the illiterate sixteen-year-old who works in your customer service department.

Name _____

Old Folks' Home Address _____

Please debit my credit card £49.95 (or equivalent in the old money) weekly for the rest of my life

PLEASE TICK HERE ____ if you wish unscrupulous antiques dealers to visit you and buy your family heirlooms for cash at knockdown prices because "there's no demand for this style any more".

ORDER NOW to receive these super free gifts!
* A certificate of authenticity
* A St Ninian Bookmark
* A 'Life of St Ninian' wall chart
* The Wee Guide to St Ninian

And some other stuff we knocked up on the iMac at work

OUR 30-DAY MONEY BACK GUARANTEE *was also knocked up on the iMac. In ten seconds flat.*

TV Guide

8.0   **Columba**   ***PICT OF THE DAY***
Another mystery for the glass-eyed 'tec as he tries to bring Christianity to 6th-century Scotland. This week: trouble for Columba as some holy relics go missing from a monastery. Iona's crumple-coated Christian can't track them down. Is it the Vikings again, or does glamorous divorcee Mrs Polenta Brabantia know more than she's saying? Either way, the Gaelic gumshoe is in for a rough ride.

SCOTLAND INVADED

The Angles of south Britain yesterday began their most concerted attack on Scotland yet. For some years they have been pushing northwards from Northumberland in their ceaseless quest for breathing room. Now the capital Dun Eidyn has been occupied, and it is thought that the Northumbrian forces mean to press on north, intending to control the Picts who occupy this region.

Guerrilla raiding parties have been sent into the occupied area and a major offensive is planned by the Picts to protect their territory.

The Easter Bunny Always Rings Twice

Christians have been complaining recently about the almost constant chocolate diet they have to put up with. 'We're having to celebrate Easter twice,' complained one regular church goer, 'and to be honest it's not just the cost but we really are getting sick of chocolate eggs and simnel cake.'

Sporting the latest tonsure, a spokesman from the church explained that it wasn't their fault that the two church years had got out of sync, but they were hoping that the forthcoming Synod of Whitby would sort things out.

'What has happened is that those of us in the Celtic Church use a different calendar to that of the Anglo-Saxons. But really it is just as valid. Bede himself will admit that we worship the same thing. He will say that we held in our hearts and venerated and preached nothing other than he did, which was a very venerable thing to say.

'Anyway, spare a thought for poor old Queen Eanflaeld. When King Oswy has finished his fasting, she is still on a restricted diet and celebrating Palm Sunday. That must make her a bit tetchy, don't you think?'

9

PERTH ARENA

Skinnergate, Perth

2 March

Scotland's Toughest Saint Tag Team Contest

TRUST TWINS versus
BLACK BIBLE BASHERS

A wrestling bout to settle once and forever who
brought Christianity to Scotland.

TRUTH TWINS (Gold lamé boiler suits)
Nice Boy Ninian issued this challenge: 'We've heard how you
have claimed to have introduced Christianity to Scotland.
Well, you're stealing our glory, you're nothing but cheap liars.
We've been converting since about 403 or so.' 'Yeah,' added
Pretty Boy Palladius, who had to be held back in case he
made a mess of his hair.

BLACK BIBLE BASHERS (Black leather thongs)
'You don't scare me,' thundered Mauler Mungo. 'You're just
two-bit has-beens. Nobody's even heard of you'. 'Yeah,'
growled Crusher Columba. 'I defeated that Loch Ness
Monster with my own bare hands.'

Main Bout (21.00)

In the blue corner **TRUTH TWINS**:
St 'Nice Boy' Ninian and St 'Pretty Boy' Palladius
In the red corner **BLACK BIBLE BASHERS**:
St 'Crusher' Columba and St 'The Mauler' Mungo
No gouging, spitting, biting, croziers, or invoking God.

Bonus Bouts (20.00 and 20.30)
THE CULROSS CLAWER (St Serf)
versus THE DRAGON
Fife's favourite takes on a ravening reptile.
THE VIKINGS versus THE SOLID SAINTS
*Non-Believing Norsemen should simply slay
St Adrian and St Monan*

Pictish Stones: The Truth!

One of the great mysteries of the world has been the meaning of the enigmatic stones carved by the Picts, with mystical symbols and depictions of beasts and people, which have defied interpretation. They are simple yet complex, sophisticated yet harmonious. Do they hold the key to the secrets of the world, learnt by a people close to nature and at one with their world? These questions have puzzled academics for centuries.

So at long last after many years, well days anyway, a new work on the interpretation of Pictish symbols is about to be published. We spoke to the controversial author, Dr Ceilidh Minogue, who talked us through the findings.

'The work has been exciting and rewarding, and I am thrilled with my success. I have decoded the symbols and learnt how they put them together. What makes it even more fascinating is that they were obviously not an isolated tribe but part of a real European community. Take this sequence of symbols (I have put them all into the modern idiom).

The groups of symbols read:

- Cup of boiled heather (3 copper pieces) with dried kale (5 copper pieces)
- For unhurried service, visit tasty Triduana for VIP treatment (Rescobie XXVI)
- We do **NOT** have hot chocolate
- Pigs, livestock and slaves must not be brought into the main bar
- Closed until 3 May 2020 because of Foot and Mouth
- No salesmen, reps or saints
- Now wash your hands
- Axes must be left at reception
- No tribal colours
- No spitting on the Saxons

This is quite an interesting one with a suggestion of humour:

- Go away – we gave at the office

It is good to know that there are some universal truths that leap the gap of time, gushed Dr Minogue.

Get Out the Bunting

It looks like we're all going to be in for a treat. One of the great holy men of God will be visiting Scotland. We've just heard a rumour from the Bishop of Hexham's office that Saint Andrew will be coming to Fife.

As all our readers know, Andrew was the brother of Saint Peter and he too was a fisherman. It does come as rather a surprise to us that he should be making the journey, as he must be very old by now. But then he is a saint and no doubt God has blessed him with long life. (Perhaps He'll do the same for the milk some time?)

We're campaigning for the day of his visit to be one of feasting. When do we ordinary people get a chance to really celebrate something truly Godsent? Let's all have street parties and wear our gaudiest clothes. We'll be giving away free Saltires to wave. Let's line the highways of the realm and give a big warm-hearted Pictish welcome to everyone's favourite holy man, Saint Andrew.

On behalf of all our fellow citizens we have also decided to lobby the King to make the 30th November a public holiday forever to celebrate this once-in-a-life-time visit, and maybe name a town in Fife after him.

Erratum: We'd like to apologise for the erroneous information we reported about Saint Andrew. Our correspondent got a little carried away and neglected to check his sources. As many of our readers did point out, not only would he have to be long lived but also capable of resurrection since he was martyred at Patras. Instead, it is his relics that will be coming to Scotland. The King has added that you can celebrate if you want, but it's not going to be a public holiday.

SCOTLAND INVADED

The Viking invasion of Scotland began in earnest yesterday as Iona was ransacked, its abbey plundered and its community butchered. Norse raids on the country have become more common in recent years, but this latest atrocity suggests the Vikings intend to settle here permanently.

More news as it happens.

Endless Reign – King Constantine II

900 'So have you heard the great news, Donald, we've got a new king!'

'A new king? You don't say, Andrew. It's good to see a new face on the coins.'

902 News travels fast in the kingdom of Scotland. By the end of the year, anyone who was anyone had heard and were practising their bows, perfecting their curtsies and dusting down their hessian leggings in the hope of being invited to the coronation of Constantine II.

910 'He's living to a grand old age, this king of ours.'

'Aye, Andrew, a fine upstanding looking man. It's a blessing for the country that he is in good health. I suppose it is good to have some stability in Scotland. But on the other hand, it is a bit dull just having the same king all the time.'

923 October. **NEWS FLASH.** The king has a cold. Courtiers and his cousin Malcolm are very worried about his health. Will he survive? Experts have been working day and night with infusions of herbs. Prayer specialists have been up since dawn, praying. But will it be to no avail? It would be a tragedy if he were taken from us so young. Funeral plans are well advanced. Insiders say that the preferred options seems to be either a Viking style burning of the corpse, perhaps on a boat if we're lucky, or the body being carried by a grief-stricken family, wailing and weeping, to its last resting place in a specially designed tomb on Iona.

923 November. *Court Circular.* After a brief sniffle, King Constantine has returned to his duties. The king will be opening a new hovel development outside Perth. The queen will be attending a pig-naming ceremony.

931 King Constantine still rules. The long-lived king still sits on the throne. Reports have come in that some factions are suggesting that if he won't die of natural causes someone should give him a hand.

Other News. Reports of sudden and unexplained deaths hitting the nobility of Scotland. A spokesman for the king said that Constantine was shaken by the news of these terrible and sudden tragedies. He is saddened that so many of his close friends should no longer be around the court joking and plotting. A great loss, said the king.

937 May. Reports have been coming in of the sad death of King Constantine at the hands of the barbarous Athelstane. The king had gone down to Brunanburgh to fight off the Saxons. Although the whole nation grieves, he had had a good innings. So who's going to be king now? The clever money is on his cousin Malcolm, although maybe one of his sons (they're certainly old enough now) could be crowned. Yes, wipe away your tears and get ready for a good knees-up to celebrate.

937 June. Welcome back to king Constantine. Yes, although the country suffered great loss of life at the battle of Brunanburgh, the king survived. The oat harvest looks like being good this year, the sheep have had a successful spring lambing and wool should be cheaper this year. Fishermen report good stocks of herring.

943 Thank God for that. At last! The king has resigned. After 43 years we finally get to see a new face on throne. It really is about time. The ordinary 10th-century citizen doesn't have the patience for these long reigns. Let's ring the changes a bit more regularly in the future.

From 843, which is generally accepted to be when the Picts and Scots got together, until 1058 when Malcolm Canmore came to the throne, there were 19 kings on the throne in just over 200 years. Bearing in mind that Constantine II ruled for 43 years, on average the others ruled for under 10.

Scots' Bad Teeth Blamed for Earl's Death

Norse dentists today slammed Scotland's atrocious record of dental health and hygiene, blaming them for the terrible demise of Sigurd, Earl of Orkney. Earl Sigurd had been holidaying in Moray, fought the Scots and as ever won. Maelbrigit, some low-born Scots chief, was captured and beheaded, although he had especially nasty dental problems. Sigurd tied the head to his saddle, to show the bairns and as a trophy for the mantelpiece. But as he rode along, the severed head of Maelbrigit with its buck teeth bit into his leg, breaking the skin. The wound festered and Sigurd died in agony from blood poisoning.

Thistle Do Us!

Scottish fighters were saved from Norse marauders yesterday – by the humble thistle. The Scots were sleeping near Luncarty, unaware that enemies were planning an attack. The Norsemen intended to sneak up on the defenceless Scottish force and slay them in the night. However, the Norse noddles stumbled into a patch of thistles and their cries woke the sleepers. The Scots defended themselves and the Scandinavians were driven off. There are already calls for the thistle to be recognised as a Scottish emblem, perhaps by commemoration on a coin marking the event.

Kincardine Woman Wins Award to Industry

Finella, wife of the Mormaer of the Mearns, has been given a prestigious award for innovation.

'Finella has made huge advances in mechanics, ballistics, toxicology and the new science of robotics,' said Kenneth MacSemiconductor for Scottish Enterprise 1000. 'We are happy to sponsor this new enterprise with a bucket load of gold.'

Her contraption, the 'King's Apple', is a splendid clockwork machine. When the apple is moved, golden angels with loaded crossbows whirl round. King Kenneth III of Scots is to present the award at Green Castle, near Fettercairn.

It has not always been such happy days at Green Castle. Only recently Finella's son was slain, and King Kenneth was blamed by some.

Breaking News
Kenneth III, King of Scots, is slain, foully murdered by a machine that shot poisoned arrows. Finella it to blame.

'This is shocking news,' said Kenneth MacSemiconductor for Scottish Enterprise 1000. 'How will we get our gold back?'

The Tragedy of Macbeth

by William Shakespeare

First draft

Macbeth is this Scottish bloke who wants to be king. The only way he can do this is to murder Duncan, the present king, a benevolent wise monarch (OK, I took a few liberties: he was actually a bit of drip). Lots of bad things then happen. James I should like it as there's lots of witches and prophecies, and luckily his line goes through Duncan. Lady Macbeth is Macbeth's wife (should I give her a name?): not sure what to do with her. The plot so far is that Macbeth is considering murdering Duncan in his castle and usurping the throne.

MACBETH. If it were done when 'tis done, then 'twere well
   It were done quickly. If the assassination
   Could trammel up the consequence, and catch,
   With his surcease, success; that but this blow
   Might be the be-all and the end-all -here,
   But here, upon this bank and shoal of time,
   We'ld jump the life to come. But in these cases
   We still have judgement here, that we but teach
   Bloody instructions, which being taught return
   To plague the inventor. This even-handed justice
   Commends the ingredients of our poison'd chalice
   To our own lips. He's here in double trust:
   First, as I am his kinsman and his subject,
   Strong both against the deed; then, as his host,
   Who should against his murtherer shut the door,
   Not bear the knife myself. Besides, this Duncan
   Hath borne his faculties so meek, hath been
   So clear in his great office, that his virtues
   Will plead like angels trumpet-tongued against
   The deep damnation of his taking-off,
   And pity, like a naked new-born babe
   Striding the blast, or heaven's cherubin horsed
   Upon the sightless couriers of the air,
   Shall blow the horrid deed in every eye,
   That tears shall drown the wind. I have no spur
   To prick the sides of my intent, but only
   Vaulting ambition, which o'erleaps itself
   And falls on the other.

       Enter Lady Macbeth.

 How now, what news?
LADY MACBETH. He has almost supp'd.
 Why have you left the chamber?

MACBETH. Hath he ask'd for me?
LADY MACBETH. Know you not he has?
MACBETH. We will proceed no further in this business:
  He hath honor'd me of late, and I have bought
  Golden opinions from all sorts of people,
  Which would be worn now in their newest gloss,
  Not cast aside so soon.
LADY MACBETH. Aye, you're right, let's talk no more on 't
  How about a few beers and a shag?
MACBETH. All right.

The End

A Guide to Life in 1065

Part of a series of helpful hints to life in Scotland

Life is hard here in Scotland and there are many ways to meet your maker. Starvation is a very common cause of death. Food is short even in good years and none of it seems to have much nutrition in it: a diet of leaves and grass, for example, tends to be short of a few essential vitamins.

Here in the Highlands, there is the almost constant possibility of violent death. The seemingly endless internecine fights, pub brawls, border raids, or full-scale wars limit the chances of making it even to middle age. For as we all know, fighting can shorten the life of even the most canny of men.

Disease is rife here since we don't have a particularly good sewerage system. I think we can safely blame that on the Romans. Everywhere else in Europe seemed to get a decent sanitation system from the Romans except us!

And of course hypothermia has a habit of parting you far earlier than you expected from your loved ones.

So, what can you do to ensure that you have a long and as fruitful a life as possible?

Our advice is that the best thing you can do to preserve your life in Scotland is to move somewhere else! We suggest Hastings; it's a quiet out of the way place. It's near the sea so the air is fresh and wholesome. Let's face it, it's the sort of place that nothing happens, where the most excitement in a day is when some spotty farm lad slips over in the pig shed and the strong smell of East Sussex boar spoils his night out with the baker's daughter. Yes, go to Hastings: nothing ever happens there and nothing ever will!

SCOTLAND INVADED

Yet again. We think it's the French, but we'll let you know.

How to Get A Head

It was a sad day in 1093 when the beloved queen Margaret died. She had acquired a reputation for goodness and piety, and was renowned for helping the needy and infirm. She was responsible for the establishment (or re-establishment) of abbeys at Dunfermline and Iona. She married Malcolm Canmore (Malcolm III: he who usurped the good Macbeth and was son of the feeble Duncan), and bore him six sons: Edward, Ethelred, Edmund, Edgar, Alexander and David: four of whom would be kings (although only briefly in Edmund's case). Edward was killed with his father at Alnwick earlier in 1093, and on hearing of their deaths, Margaret also died.

Margaret is generally credited with increasing the influence of the English and Continent in Scotland; indeed, of being a civilising influence (if indeed the Scotland of the time needed civilising). She may have been born in Hungary, but was in England when the Normans invaded in 1066. She and her brother, Edgar the Atheling, fled to Scotland. It is true that she influenced the church, but it should be remembered that Malcolm Canmore had spent many years in England while Macbeth was king, only taking the Scottish throne with southern help, while Edgar was similarly placed on the throne by the English.

Margaret was buried at the abbey she founded at Dunfermline. Her life story and an account of her pious works was recorded by her biographer Turgot, and the good woman was made a saint in 1250 as her renown grew and miracles were associated with her relics. Her shrine was visited by thousands of pilgrims, and she is the only Scottish saint to be universally venerated in the Roman calendar.

Her rest, however, was interrupted at the Reformation. Fearing that her shrine would be desecrated, the last abbot of Dunfermline Abbey removed her remains (and those of Malcolm) to Madrid in Spain. The Jesuits at Douai acquired her head.

Scottish Journeys

You won't be getting me in one of those carts; they look awfie rickity to me. I prefer to keep my erse on the back of a good sturdy pony. But I can tell you this wee beastie is a marvel. Why, when I had to walk, it would take me a day at least and I could only carry two stone of turnips but now, well can you guess how much I've got here. Why, it's nearly three stone, almost a third more. My wife says that if I wasn't such a lazy fat bastard I could shift ten stone each journey.

Feeling Pious? Why Not Build An Abbey ...

It costs less than you believe, and just think of the souls you save.

It's all the rage these days. It started with Queen Margaret (now our very own SAINT MARGARET since 1250) at Dunfermline and Iona. Then Alexander I built Inchcolm, after being washed onto the island during the storm, and Scone.

But now David I has really taken a lead, founding abbeys at Holyrood (apparently after a miraculous escape from a stag in the royal park), Jedburgh, Kelso, Melrose, Kinloss, Newbattle, Dundrennan, and Cambuskenneth. Many other abbeys and priories are also being founded during his reign by the noblemen of Scotland.

So get involved and build an abbey today. These fine and elegant buildings have at their hearts a great awe-inspiring church where seven services are celebrated each day, and where prayers can be said for you and your loved ones. Beside this is the cloister, a courtyard surrounded by a walk, with ranges of buildings housing a refectory, dormitory, chapter house

(where the business of the abbey is managed), sacristy (holding the vestments and treasures) and storage. Abbeys are not only great centres of Christianity, but also great money-making enterprises, although unfortunately all the cash stays with the Church.

So build an abbey today. All you need is a quite of lot of land and a large pot of gold for buildings and all the trimmings. A small price to pay for an eternity in paradise. This will be a lasting testament to you and your family, where prayers will be said for your soul for the rest of time*.

Issued by the Abbey Marketing Board.

*Disclaimer. The rest of time is believed to mean until Judgement Day. While all care has been taken to ensure that your abbey survives until then, we take no responsible for invasions by Vikings or English, earthquakes and lightning strikes, acts of God, or unforeseen occurrences such as John Knox and the Reformation which could really bugger things up.

History Is Not What It Used to Be ... Thank God!

While the rest of the economy is booming, it was reported today that many historians, bards and chroniclers are being forced out of work. There is simply not enough history to go around.

'It is sad,' said a spokesman, 'at least for these individuals who used to be employed as storytellers and entertainers. Apart from a few skirmishes with Vikings, nothing much is happening. Even the Battle of Largs was a bit of an anticlimax. Loads of Viking longboats, but then up comes a storm and only a few of them land. They are seen off by some beachcombers and a party of Girl Guides. Indeed, I can't remember the last time a king died of unnatural causes. It's great to live in a time of prosperity. I predict that in 600 years we will be one of the richest parts of Europe.'

The good news started with Kings Edgar, Alexander and David, sons of Margaret and Malcolm Canmore. These sensible fellows were more interested in building abbeys and good relations with our neighbours than all that pointless fighting. Malcolm the Maiden and William the Lyon may have made a few mistakes, but again everything has been going nicely.

Alexander II, the old king, was great, and then our present monarch Alexander III has actually taken the Hebrides for Scotland from the Vikings, while maintaining excellent relations with England. Hurrah. That is one in the eye with a sharp stick with a barbed point for all those moaning minnies whingeing about the lack of a good war.

Our only slight worry is the absence of an heir ...

Alexander the Dead

Well, that's our king dead: have these kings no sense of direction? Wandering off to have a quickie with the wife. If he spent more time thinking about ruling his country and less time about sex, the rest of us wouldn't be looking down the barrel of a mangonel.

The worst thing of it is that he wasn't a bad king. He taught those Vikings a bit of a lesson near Largs and then signed the Treaty of Perth with them and acquired the Western Isles. That was a good bit of business since we never sent them any money but they stayed away anyway. We still have a few sniggers about that in the pub after we've put the paper to bed. But one shouldn't gloat since Scotland's in a right pickle now.

Edward, the king of England, is breathing down our necks so we need some radical solution that will keep Scotland together and at the same town placate a man who is best described as bloodthirsty.

Since there are two main contenders to replace Alexander III, most experts agree that there should be a middle candidate. The general opinion suggests that Margaret, Alexander the ex-king's three-year granddaughter, also known as the Maid of Norway, would be the best choice. It would appear that Edward would be OK about that. In fact, he has hinted that if Margaret married his son then we might actually have peace in our time. So let's get her over here and settle down to prosperity. Let's get back to building abbeys and alliances.

Choice of New King is a Stitch-up, Claim Protesters

Edward I of England has chosen a new Scottish king who is little more than a figurehead, claim critics.

Following the death of Margaret, Maid of Norway, there were fears that civil war could divide the country. With 13 claimants to the throne, Bishop Fraser, one of the Guardians of Scotland, appealed to Edward I of England to select the best candidate. Edward narrowed the competition down to a short list of two:

• Robert Bruce. Patriot, nationalist and hero, Bruce is widely fancied as the people's choice

• John Balliol, whose main qualification for the job seems to be his acceptance of the English king as his Overlord, Superior and Lord Paramount of Scotland.

Now Edward's selection of John Balliol has drawn criticism from those who say his choice of king is intended to instal a puppet ruler in Scotland, and that the country will really be ruled from England.

TV Guide

9.0   **Crimewatch**
        In 1296, the town of Berwick was invaded and 16,000 of its
        inhabitants slaughtered. Eyewitnesses claim an army of 35,000
        troops marched into Berwick and sacked the town, killing men,
        women and children and leaving devastation in their wake.
        Informants have suggested Edward I of England may be
        responsible. Were you in the vicinity around 1296? Did you
        see anything? Do you know anything?
        We're waiting for your help.
        Call V V V VI I IX VIII

HAMMER BANGS ON

Edward I has condemned the Scottish nation for their obstinacy and refusal to accept him as overlord of Scotland.

In an exclusive statement he made to his hairdresser while getting a trim, the brutal monarch spoke frankly about his reign of terror and incursions into Scotland.

'The stubborn Scots won't take the hint!' moaned the monarch. 'I destroy Berwick-upon-Tweed and they do nothing. But put vinegar on the chips instead of sauce, and they go berserk!'

Edward, the Hammer of the Scots, is no stranger to criticism of his policies. His execution of William Wallace in 1305 was widely seen as the most brutal public death of recent times and has led to some commentators predicting that Wallace will be seen as a martyr and a symbol of Scottish independence. The 'Butcher of Berwick' is unrepentant.

'It's true I have adopted a scorched-earth policy. But let's face it, you can't tell much difference between before and after. Well, what's a few burnt-out villages? They leave old carriage wheels lying about their gardens. And prams.'

Then his hairdresser said: 'Something for the weekend, sir?' and Edward snapped: 'The Scottish throne would do, fool', before storming out without leaving a tip.

21

The Scots Wha Hae

BRAVEHEART BOARD GAME

Rules

You will need a dice, and a marker for each player. (Some bit of old tat from a cracker will do, or a small cube of cheese.) Place your markers at the start and take turns to throw the dice. Each time you throw, move along the number of squares represented by the number on the dice. Remember to paint your face with a saltire for that authentic Braveheart look.

The winner is the first person to die a martyr's death, ensuring his name will live for evermore in the annals of Scottish independence and the liberty of her people and will be a bright flame of inspiration to Scotland's national pride etc etc.

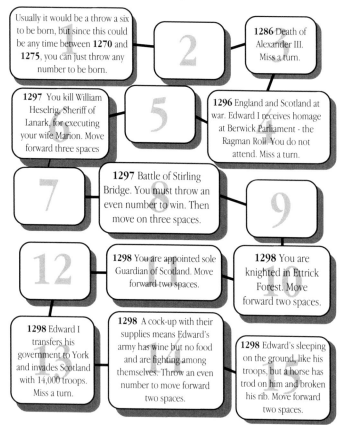

Usually it would be a throw a six to be born, but since this could be any time between **1270** and **1275**, you can just throw any number to be born.

2

1286 Death of Alexander III. Miss a turn.

1297 You kill William Heselrig, Sheriff of Lanark, for executing your wife Marion. Move forward three spaces

5

1296 England and Scotland at war. Edward I receives homage at Berwick Parliament - the Ragman Roll. You do not attend. Miss a turn.

7

1297 Battle of Stirling Bridge. You must throw an even number to win. Then move on three spaces.

9

12

1298 You are appointed sole Guardian of Scotland. Move forward two spaces.

1298 You are knighted in Ettrick Forest. Move forward two spaces.

1298 Edward I transfers his government to York and invades Scotland with 14,000 troops. Miss a turn.

1298 A cock-up with their supplies means Edward's army has wine but no food and are fighting among themselves. Throw an even number to move forward two spaces.

1298 Edward's sleeping on the ground, like his troops, but a horse has trod on him and broken his rib. Move forward two spaces.

1298 English cavalry routs Scottish force at Battle of Falkirk. Hundreds of Scots die. It is a major tactical defeat. Miss a turn.

17

1298 You resign your Guardianship and are replaced by Robert the Bruce and John Comyn. Miss a turn.

18

1300 You swan about Europe on 'diplomatic missions'. Oh, and pressure from the Pope and the French forces Edward to sign a truce. Move on two places.

1299 The Scots recapture Stirling Castle, and you go on holiday to the Continent, or something. Move forward two spaces.

19

20

21

1302 Back to Scotland. More problems with Edward. Miss a turn.

22

1303 Start leading attacks on English garrisons in Scotland (a man needs a hobby) with varying success. Throw an odd number to move on a space, an even number to stay in the same space.

23

1304 You are defeated at Happrew, Stirling Castle falls to the English, you become a fugitive. Miss a turn.

24

1305 The English hang, draw and quarter you. You are disembowelled, after horrible torture, while still alive in front of a huge crowd in London. You wouldn't have the breath to cough, never mind cry 'Freedom!' Nevertheless, throw a six, and you will ensure your name lives on for all time as a true patriot and hero of Scotland, and you will win this game.

26

1304 You are betrayed by Menteith and captured by the English. It's not your day. However things aren't all bad - you get a free throw as soon as you land on this space. Unfortunately it only leads to...

25

William Wallace, Guardian of the Kingdom of Scotland and commander of its armies, in the name of the renowned Prince, Lord John, by the grace of God illustrious King of Scotland, by consent of the Community of that realm

Robert the Bruce Heirloom Edition Collectible Bear

Robert the Bruce A legendary name in Scottish history and a tireless campaigner for Scottish independence. Now immortalised in the Robert the Bruce **Heirloom Edition Collectible Bear.**

Bruce 's efforts drove the English totally out of Scotland. Now you can fight the good fight in your own home with this high-quality bear. With tartan sash, loveable furry ears and blue face, he captures all of Bruce 's dignity and magnetism.

Any resemblance to the William Wallace Heirloom Edition Collectible Bear is complete coincidence

Commemorate His Bravery

Robert the Bruce

.... This Collectible Bear

Need to delete all references to William Wallace

features detachable heart in realistic catgut.

Victor of Bannockburn

Coming Soon
The Lorraine Kelly Heirloom Edition Collectible Bear

About the Artist
Morag Bean was brought up in a cave in Galloway and started her career robbing and eating passing travellers. She developed an interest in soft toys when she began to make crude effigies out of human skin. She has now risen to the top of her profession as a maker of fine quality collectible bears, shaped like famous Scots.

Celebrity **AGONY** Column

Dear Mr Bruce

I've been having a bit of trouble with my next door neighbour, George Tuppence. There's a patch of land at the bottom of my garden, which I've used for some 20 years. I grow cauliflower and other brassica on it. George says it is his and once he made a rude remark to me over the fence. The atmosphere is now quite difficult and we no longer discuss the football with each other but restrict ourselves to comments about the weather. What should I do, to ease this situation?

Unsettled

Dear Unsettled

Invite your neighbour out for a wee chat. I suggest somewhere neutral: the town hall or the kirk maybe. Then stab him to death.

Yours, Robert. King.

P. S. And any relatives with him, as they can be a real hassle later.

TV Guide   Pick of the Day

2.30 **Carry On Bruce**

If at first you don't succeed, buy her a bunch of flowers! The Carry On Team take liberties – er, with history – by showing the Bruce as a lovable conman who finds himself married to both Joan Sims and Barbara Windsor. Will they find out, or can Sid give them both a bit – er, of the Scottish crown? Meanwhile the scheming Edward I won't rest til he's got it – er, rule of Scotland.

Classic Scene

Watch for the moment when Sid James asks Charlie Hawtrey, 'Where is the Hammer of the Scots?' and Charlie chirps, 'Here!' bringing a mallet down on Sid's fingers.

Cast

Robert the Bruce	SID JAMES
Isabel of Mar	JOAN SIMS
Elizabeth de Burgh	BARBARA WINDSOR
Walter, the High Steward	CHARLES HAWTREY
David II	BERNARD BRESSLAW
Edward I	KENNETH WILLIAMS

25

Battered and Bruced

A rather sorry looking Edward II spoke to us on his way home from Bannockburn near Stirling.

You don't look very happy Mr Edward the Second?

'You're right there. This trip has been a bit of a disappointment to be honest. I came up here with pretty high hopes of quelling a few rebellious Scots. I'm not the soldier my dad was, but I had a reasonable army and some good officers. But it looks like I'm going home with my bottom tanned.'

So, what do you think went wrong Ted?

'To be honest, I think I'm just a bit of a useless military leader. Fair game to old Bob Bruce. He didn't do anything wrong. But I rather threw the battle away. I don't know what I was thinking of, fighting on such a narrow front. I mean, playing into his hands or what?

'Oh well, that's it for me. I'm going home to a nice hot bath and a glass of wine. I don't think I'll be coming up here to fight again. It's all a bit rough and one of the gentlemen on the other side made some very rude gestures in my direction when he saw me.'

A surprisingly honest appraisal of events from the current king of England. We'll say goodbye to him and maybe catch a word with Brucie.

Hello there Mr Bruce, anything to say to our readers?

'We bloody stuffed them. That was a great fight. But I'm so drunk now. You know I'm drunk. Can you tell? Scotland! Scotland! We are the champions!

'You're my best friend, do you know that?!?'

We left the victorious King of Scots and a few of his mates in the Cross Keys celebrating a famous victory

Hulloo! Magazine presents
THOSE CRAZY STEWART BROTHERS!

We visit the three royal Stewart brothers: KING ROBERT III OF SCOTS; ROBERT, STEWART, Duke of Albany; and ALEXANDER STEWART, Earl of Buchan.

We discuss their lives – their dreams – their hopes for the future.

Hulloo! Magazine: Robert III, King of Scots and great-grandson of Robert the Bruce, came to the throne in 1390. Robert not only has a kingdom to manage, but was seriously injured in a riding accident in 1388 and lost David, his son and heir, in 1402. Robert, Duke of Albany, his younger brother, made Chamberlain of the kingdom in 1382, often likes to help-out his royal brother in affairs of state. Alexander, Earl of Buchan, is the youngest of the three. He also likes to aid his brother in bringing the rebellious Highlands under control. We visit artistic King Robert in his great castle of Rothesay on Bute, before moving on to the imposing Robert, Duke of Albany, at Doune, and finally roguish Alexander at Lochindorb.

HULLOO!: Robert is not the name you were christened with, is it?

RKoS: No, I was known as John.

HULLOO!: Why was it changed?

RKoS: People thought that John was unlucky because of bad things that had happened to John Balliol and King John of England. They thought that Robert would be better. It wasn't. Woe is me.

HULLOO!: OK. Tell me about your disability.

RKoS: You mean the melancholy and depression?

HULLOO!: Er, no. I meant the riding accident.

RKoS: Oh that. I got kicked by a horse. It left me lame. Both physically and mentally and spiritually.

HULLOO!: Ah ha. You are a great lover of justice, though.

RKoS: I guess so. There is precious little of that in Scotland at this time. I know I should do something about it. My brother, Robert, is ruling things for me. Not that I asked him to, exactly. My son David might have done a good job if he hadn't died like that, quite suddenly.

HULLOO!: It must have been a tragedy.

RKoS: Yes, my brother Robert obviously felt David needed to lose some weight. So he put him on a crash diet at Falkland.

HULLOO!: You have another son, James. He's going to France soon.

RKoS: I have much regard for James. I believe he will form a new dynasty of Jameses. But he's looking a bit portly, a bit thick around the midriff. My brother has been eyeing him up.

HULLOO!: I see. But you must have high hopes for the future?

RKoS: Hardly, I came to Rothesay to die.

HULLOO!: Oh.

RKoS: Yes, I want my epitaph to read: 'The worst of kings and the most miserable of men.'

HULLOO!: Thanks for your time.

Hulloo! Magazine: We travel to Doune in the heart of Scotland to talk to Robert Stewart, Duke of Albany.

HULLOO!: Robert is the name you were christened with?

RDoA: Aye, it is. A fine name, I say.

HULLOO!: It must have been difficult always being in the shadow of your brother, knowing that one day he would be king. Then he even took your name.

RDoA: No, I never had any problem. I have always done my best to rule in his stead, er, and to help him as much as possible. Someone needs to. I have been Governor since 1398. I like to think I have done a fine job.

HULLOO!: It was good of you to take care of the king's son David.

RDoA: What! Who have you been talking to? What have they been saying?

HULLOO!: You know, at Falkland. Your brother said that David was looking a bit obese so you put him on a diet.

RDoA: Oh, yes. We maybe overdid it a bit when David passed away and died like that. A terrible shame! Luckily I was here to take even more power.

HULLOO!: That's good. Mind you, with your brother the king predicting his own death, his son James could soon be king.

RDoA: Wouldn't we welcome the day. We can only wish James the best on his journey to France, and hope beyond hope that nobody lets the English know so that they capture him and imprison him until 1424 leaving me to be king in everything but name. Oh no, I say.

HULLOO!: Indeed, and thank you for your time.

Hulloo! Magazine: We go to Lochindorb in the remote Highlands to interview Alexander, Earl of Buchan.

HULLOO!: How do you find it here in this wild part of Scotland.

AEoB: I rather like it, dear girl. It is good to get away from all those petty rules. My, you are a fine-looking young filly.

HULLOO!: Er, yes. You are lord of Badenoch and Earl of Buchan.

AEoB: That's correct. I acquired the earldom through my wife, Isabella.

HULLOO!: You had a whirlwind romance, but have since separated.

AEoB: Alas, celebrity marriages: they never last. The earldom's nice, though.

HULLOO!: You have a reputation as a bit of a lady's man. I believe the Bishop of Moray has been, er, a little critical.

AEoB: So I hear, dear girl. But those of the cloth just don't understand.

HULLOO!: And now they are blaming you for fire damage done to Forres and Elgin, and have excommunicated you.

AEoB: I know, I know, dreadful, isn't it? We just went there for a couple of drinks, and then before you know it there's fire everywhere, and the cathedral's been burnt to the ground. Should have taken it easier with the Whisky slammers.

HULLOO!: Some have even called you the 'Wolf of Badenoch'. Doesn't that make you angry?

AEoB: No, not at all. I've had a great life. And I even have a splendid tomb lined up in Dunkeld Cathedral. Anyway, call me Wolfie. Everyone else does.

HULLOO!: Thank you very much and could you take your hand off my knee.

It Wasn't Fair

James I tells us about his time in England.

The last 18 years have been tough, I can tell you. I was only 12 when I was captured by Henry IV of England and held hostage. He kept me prisoner all that time. It really wasn't fair. I should have been king of Scotland; instead I had to moulder away in a well-kept, draught-free palace full of rich tapestries, wearing gold-embroidered robes and fur cloaks. There was nothing to do except get a sound education. I mean, I may be a scholar and I have learnt to be a skilful musician, but is that compensation for being away from a creaky rotten old castle out in the wilds of the North away from any civilisation? Does having access to one of the most glittering courts in Europe really balance against living in your own country where there are savages round every corner and most of the population are stricken by poverty and disease?

I never got to go anywhere either, unless all the servants and army and nobles and knights went too. I suppose I did get to go to France when Henry was fighting some big battle. It was really exciting, all those archers and the siege engines. It was so disciplined.

Er, I mean it was awful, and the English didn't seem to know anything. The whole experience was a nightmare.

Don't Call Me 'Jimmy'!

Address to the nation.

I'm back in Scotland. And I'm your new king! Call me James I. Now that I'm in charge things are going to change!

There's too much lawlessness. You bloody savages need to be taught a lesson. Separating the heads of the Duke of Albany, his sons, and the Earl of Lennox from their respective bodies is a good start. Damnable traitors!

This country is a disgrace. It's in a mess. For one thing Parliament has been very lazy. They're going to have to get their erses in gear. I want legislation and I want it now! I want a system to settle civil disputes, I want more democracy in Parliament, and I don't like heresy.

People may mutter about personal freedom. But they can bite my bum. Football and poaching are banned. There's going to be price fixing in the hostelries. I want the country to grow up and be a bit more responsible. And if you don't do what I say, there'll be a few more men shorter by a head.

Breaking News

James I has been murdered by Sir Robert Graham in Perth following discontent with James's heavy-handed policies. Following an old tradition, James's heart is to be removed from his body and taken on pilgrimage to the Holy Land. Hopefully some kind Knight of St John will bring it back.

29

SEARCH FOR MISSING PEER

Mystery continues to surround the recent disappearance of Lord Glamis and his friend the 'Tiger' Earl of Crawford.

Investigators are baffled as to how the peer could vanish from his stronghold, Glamis Castle in the Vale of Strathmore, without servants seeing him. He was last seen late on a Saturday night, when all the doors were locked.

Eyewitnesses claim Lord Glamis and the Earl of Crawford were playing cards all evening and had had quite a lot to drink. Shouting and bawdy singing could be heard coming from the room. A servant visited them close to the witching hour to warn them that it was not wise to gamble on the Sabbath, as the Devil could claim their souls. It is believed that he was driven away with curses as the gamblers vowed to play on 'until the crack of doom' or words to that effect.

This would not be the first time the hell-raising Lord Glamis has played with danger. A few years ago he refused to cross a gypsy's palm with silver. And he has been known to go to bed without saying his prayers. But playing cards on a Sunday is his most death-defying stunt yet.

Rumours that he may have fled to South America have been dismissed as 'fantasy' by members of his family, as South America has not been discovered yet, except by people living there, of course.

Why Isn't the Man Who Built This Death Trap in Prison?

Young orphan James III was complaining today. 'It's ridiculous. A king should be able to go about his daily business, besieging a castle in safety. Exploding cannons shouldn't be something he has to worry about. I think the family could bear it better if it was an enemy cannon. But this was one of ours.'

'What I want to know is why the cannon maker has not been hauled up before the beak and given a severe ticking off: before they chop him in quarters and feed him to the dogs.'

'It's a highly unsatisfactory business. Where does it leave me? I'm only nine and I've got many earls and nobles with ambitions, thronewise. My mother, Queen Joan, and Bishop Kennedy are meant to be looking after things. But let's face it, recovering Berwick while there was a civil war in England has really annoyed Edward IV. Will there be a kingdom left for me to rule by the time they've finished?

'Must make sure I have a longer and deeper relationship with my own son.'

James IV Productions presents

THE LORD OF THE ISLES

Can good prevail?
Can right overcome?
Can James defeat the evil
Lord of the Isles?

In an age of terror, only one man can save
the world, only one man can travel to the
Black Tower of Finlaggan and confront the
Lord of the Isles in his darkling fortress.

A lowly king of Scots must stand against
the Lord's foul creatures, the evil slavering
Gaels. He must battle the elements, magic,
monsters, and his need to sleep with every
female he meets, armed only with the
truth, justice, and an overwhelmingly huge
army.

JAMES IV   Sean Connery   LORD OF THE ISLES   Christopher Lee
MARGARET OF ENGLAND   Gail Porter   SIR ANDREW WOOD   Ewan MacGregor
EARL OF ANGUS   Sir Ian McKellen   GAELS   Orcs

Shot entirely in Middle Earth except for Mordor
which was filmed at Grangemouth.

Hulloo! Magazine presents
My Imprisonment HELL! by John, Lord of the Isles

We visit John MacDonald, formerly Lord of the Isles and one of the most powerful men in Scotland, at Paisley Abbey where he has been imprisoned since 1493.

We discuss his life – his dreams – his hopes for the future.

Hulloo! Magazine: John's life has been a constant battle against the Scottish Crown to assert what he sees as the right of his people to live their lives free from interference of Scotland. Although the title Lord of the Isles has now been stripped from him, he fought valiantly until captured by James IV, King of Scots.

HULLOO!: What should I call you? What is the correct title? Mr MacDonald? Lord? John? Lord of the Isles?

JM: I don't suppose it matters now. The title has been taken from me. John will do, I guess.

HULLOO!: How do you occupy your days?

JM: I suppose it could be worse. I read, think and too often I remember. I have quite a comfortable room, I suppose, and am allowed out for some exercise most days. I am always closely watched, though, all the time.

HULLOO!: Do you manage to keep up with the latest fashions?

JM: Er, to be honest it is not much of a concern to me.

HULLOO!: So how did all this trouble start those years ago?

JM: I don't really know. We were concerned with our own affairs and tried to maintain ourselves against the Scottish kings. I think they feared us, feared our strength and the strength of our men.

HULLOO!: Yes, we hear they are really quite a rough lot.

JM: Hardly.

HULLOO!: Anyway, let us start from the beginning. You were born in the Hebrides, a pretty wild place. What was it like being brought up in a hovel of a cave with nothing to eat but earthworms and dung? I suppose at least with ten of you in a bed you would keep warm in the winter. You were lucky to survive. Tell me about that time.

JM: What are you talking about?

HULLOO!: Er, you're a Gael, aren't you? I believe it is pretty backward, even on Islay. Most of you can't speak English. There's no education or laws.

JM: Are you nuts? We are every bit as civilised and cultured as the lowland Scots. More so. Ten times more so. I had a court to rival many kings: poets, bards, sculptors, musicians, pipers, artists, doctors. We had centres of learning superior to the Continent. It's true we speak Gaelic, but I also speak English, Latin and French. My family have patronised the Church for hundreds of years, building priories and chapels. Iona was under our care. I didn't do this interview to be insulted.

HULLOO!: I am really sorry. I got the handout from James IV. Well, things must have been better in the past?

JM: I guess so.

HULLOO! How did the title Lord of the Isles come about?

JM: It was my ancestor, Somerled, in the 12th century who started the ball rolling. He was a great man and drove the Vikings out of much of the Hebrides, taking and holding their territories.

HULLOO! What became of him?

JM: He got into an argument with Malcolm the Maiden, King of Scots, and the bastard had Somerled assassinated. Somerled was so powerful that the Scots were passing bricks.

HULLOO! So has it always been difficult with the Scottish monarchy?

JM: No, but most of them were jealous and they have always been a mealy-mouthed bunch. We got on really well with Robert the Bruce: Angus Og MacDonald fought at Bannockburn and was the king's friend. He died in 1328. His son, John of Islay, was probably the first to be called 'Lord of the Isles'. We're not sure. Then later we also got the Earldom of Ross.

HULLOO!: Ooooooh, so you were nobility?

JM: Of course, you vaporous idiot. By this time we held territories right down the whole west coast of Scotland and into Argyll, and with Ross across to the east too. The Scottish Crown got more

and more worried. They tried to take Ross from us, and this came to battle at Harlaw in 1411. It was pretty bloody. We lost a lot of men, it weakened us.

HULLOO: So you entered into treasonable negotiations with the English?

JM: Listen, you fool, sometimes needs must. We didn't like the English any better than the Scots but we wanted to maintain the lordship.

HULLOO: Then James IV launched his campaign against you?

JM: Aye, that was the end. He was too powerful: I had no recourse but to surrender. Not that James is much of a general. My only hope is that he gets embroiled in a war in England, goes down to Flodden near Wooler in Northumberland, gets himself slain, and somebody ends up keeping his head as a trophy. Not that it will do as any good, and I doubt I will be sufficiently lucky to live long enough to see it.

HULLOO!: So the Lord of the Isles is no more?

JM: No, much worse. Future kings will bestow it on their eldest son. My greatest shame is knowing that in hundreds of years some jug-eared tree-hugger will have my title. I can hardly bear that.

HULLOO!: Well, to lighter things: are you going anywhere nice for your holidays?

JM: You really are an empty-headed twit. I am stuck here until I die.

The Best of Times ...
James IV

It is grand being king.

I am a good king and I tend to get on well with all the neighbouring kings. They like me and they think that I'm doing a great job. I think they are very impressed with my fleet.

My favourite ship is the Great Michael. It's huge. My pal Louis, the King of France, has even asked to borrow it. He is my special friend, even more than Henry VIII.

Actually to be honest Henry is a bit of a pain. He's always pushing his weight about. All the other kings think that too. We're going to have to teach him that you can't just go about bullying everyone and getting away with it.

Before I was king, everything was bit of a shambles here in Scotland. They were always fighting, and Dad was as bad as the rest of them.

I didn't really want to have to go into battle against him, but to be honest he'd really upset so many people that there wouldn't have been a kingdom to inherit if he'd gone on much longer. Look,

I am sad that someone killed him, that wasn't very nice at all. I bought myself an iron chain to wear just to show how sad I am.

Anyway, I've got the hang of things now and I've created what we call a 'Renaissance court'. That means we've got artists and writers and musicians, all being creative and moody.

I've also spent quite a bit of effort on organising the country, sorting out the administration and the law courts. I was also a bit fed up with the number of numpties in the court, so I've said that they all need to go to school. With a bit of luck, there won't be so many thickies hanging around with their mouths open catching flies.

Since I'd sorted out Scotland, I was going to go on a Crusade against the heretics in Turkey with Louis. But the Pope has been very mean. In fact, he and Henry seem to be ganging up against us. So I am going to take an army down to Flodden and give Henry a bit of a bloody nose.

Hee, hee, he's gone over to France so he'll have a big surprise when he comes back.

TV Guide   Pick of the Day

2.30 Carry On Mary Queen of Scots

A saucy look at sixteenth-century Scottish court intrigue with the Carry On team! Joan Sims dusts off her atrocious French accent as Mary of Guise, while Barbara Windsor's Mary Queen of Scots enrages John Knox by announcing a new game she brought over from France - 'Postman's Knox'. Sid James schemes as the Earl of Bothwell, eager to win Mary's hand and hopefully the rest of her as well. Meanwhile, Patsy Rowlands as Elizabeth I is having problems too - with her waterworks. She's never off the 'throne' long enough to sit on the throne!

Classic Scene

John Knox says, 'I am going to issue a proclamation!' and Mary replies, 'Well, don't stand upwind of me!'

Cast

Mary of Guise	JOAN SIMS
Mary, Queen of Scots	BARBARA WINDSOR
Henry, Lord Darnley	JIM DALE
James Hepburn, Earl of Bothwell	SID JAMES
Elizabeth I of England	PATSY ROWLANDS
David Rizzio	CHARLES HAWTREY
John Knox	KENNETH CONNOR
Lord Ruthven	KENNETH WILLIAMS

 Court Circular

Mary Queen of Scots will take mass in her private chapel at Holyrood and retire to her rooms. Her servant Rizzio will play music and wash her in a bath of milk. She will then go hunting to flirt wildly with the Earl of Bothwell until teatime.

The King, Henry, Lord Darnley, will seduce a stable boy and spend the afternoon rolling in the hay. He will later go on a drinking spree in the 'Stag and Scabies' tavern in the Canongate, and end up passing out in the gutter.

Patrick, Lord Ruthven, and the Earl of Morton will attend a private meeting of Scottish nobles to scheme and plot the downfall of the Queen. They will spend the evening drinking heavily and daring each other to ever more outrageous feats, until Morton dresses up as a barmaid, as part of an elaborate drinking game, and falls off the table.

The Best of Times ...

David Rizzio

It is a very grand life that God has now given me. I, David Rizzio, I whose father was a musician in Turin, now live in this wonderful country of Scotland. When I came over here I knew no one but then I met with my friend Mrs Queen of Scots. Although I am allowed to call her Mary. Now we do everything together. We go to Mass together and we go out riding together. I am with her when she rules people. It is all very good fun. Often she ask me what should she do. I tell her. I say you must stamp out all that Protestant malarkey. It is not good. All these poor people. If they continue to follow this they will all be damned. So you must make sure that they follow the Catholic faith because then they will be saved. That is what I say.

When I first came I was really lonely. Now I have many friends here in Scotland. Mr Queen of Scots is my special friend. He's really called Darnley. We are often all together and we have such fun. Some of my other special friends are Lord Ruthven and Jamie Douglas. They love to hear all about Italy. They're really interested in all the fun we used to have in Turin. They're amazed about the wide choice of meals and all the varieties of pasta. They are quite serious fellows. I try to make them smile more. I am going to try to persuade them to act in a little play I wrote for the queen.

They are coming over later this evening for a little chat about it. I hope they don't have the same Mr Grumpy faces they had on this morning when I invited them. I am going to give them some cake. Now where did I put my cake slice? Oh well I sure one of them will have a knife on them.

Knox in Locks by Mary Queen of Scots

I do not like him Knox in locks,
Said Mary Stuart, Queen of Scots,
In fact, I wish a scurvy pox,
On dratted fearsome Knox in locks.
I would not like him with the Pope,
I would not like him washed with soap,
I am quite glad he's on a boat,
I'd like him dangling on a rope.
I'm just so glad he's off at sea.
I would not like him in Dundee,
In fact he makes me quite angry,

I wouldn't have him round to tea,
They took off the chains and now he's freed
And come here spouting Calvin's Creed
That's the last thing that I need
I want the Catholics to succeed!
He doesn't like me attending mass,
He treats me like a little lass.
I think he's dull and very crass
And we all snigger when he goes past.

The Darnley Papers

I, Henry Stewart, Lord Darnley, 5th Earl of Lennox, Earl of Ross, and Duke of Albany, have decided that I shall record my thoughts and keep a diary of my life. Thus my descendants and historians will have a document of this important age. There shall be a chronicle as written by one of the great and noble men of this time.

1563. *Monday*. Nothing much has happened today. Had some breakfast. Bought a new pair of socks.

1564. *Thursday*. Going hunting again.

1565. *Saturday*. This is a bit more like it. I travel to Scotland in two days time. Must remember to pack my night-shirt and some woolly underwear. Dad says it's a bit nippy on the other side of Croydon.

1565. *Monday*. Said goodbye to Elizabeth the queen. She looked very white-faced. Did she have too much to drink at my leaving party yesterday?

1565. I have neglected my diary for many months. It's been very exciting. I met my cousin Mary. She's the queen. I thought she was quite pretty. Well, she fancied me too. In fact she liked me so much we got married. I'm unofficially king now. I shall be King Henry, I think.

1566. *Tuesday*. Coo, it's all a bit hairy. She's got a bit of temper. Some of her people at court are a bit full of themselves, all really stuck up. I haven't got on with them much. She's also got a weedy little Eyetie that keeps following us around.

1566. *March*. That bloody Italian, if he mentions his mother's home-made bloody pasta once more I'm going to stick one on him.

1566. *Wednesday*. Whoops, a bit of *faux pas* there. Got fed up listening to Neapolitan love songs and endless stories about Turin and I got carried away and killed Rizzio, that Italian. Oh well, he was only a musician. Had to apologise to Mary as she was there and the blood messed up the carpet a bit.

1566. *October*. We're going to have baby. I think we should call him Kevin or Phoenix or Chaucer but I think Mary is settled on James. God they're all called James up here. Shout out James in a crowded court and 50 people turn round.

1567. Not been too well recently. Got a bit of a problem, *down there*. Mary has been really nice and put me up in a house called Kirk o' Field. It's a bit uncomfortable with my problem so I'm wandering about in the buff. I hope no one comes in.

P. S. I was just about to stop writing when I realised that there are some rowdy youths who sound as if they are setting off fireworks. I wonder what those big barrels are for: maybe they are full of beer.

P. P. S. I had a quick peek out the window and one of them looks like that short-arsed Earl of Bothwell. I shall moon him ...

Following the runaway success* of our William Wallace collectible bear, add to the fluffy Scottish icons on your mantelpiece.

**Those twinkling eyes, that fluffy beard, those cute little ears.
Yes - it's the Terror of the Reformation.**
The Olde Rope Gallery proudly presents:

The John Knox Collectible Bear

Bear **Your Soul to God**

Who can forget how he dominated Scottish Politics and railed against the Catholic Church from the pulpit of St Giles Cathedral (*not included*). And how better to commemorate the Thundering Scot than with this love-able fellow. Who would guess that this cheeky little bear (stands 5" tall) could brutalise Mary Queen of Scots, harass the Catholic Clergy, and bully the Scottish Parliament into accepting the reformed confession of faith?

He even talks!

*Pull the string to hear a host of
John Knox phrases!*

- 'Monstrous regimen of women!'
- 'The Church of Rome is the Synagogue of Satan!'
- 'Gluttons! Wantons! Licentious Revellers!'
- 'I want a cuddle!'

ORDER FORM
Mary Queen of Scots was a slut and a whore and she got what she deserved, only not soon enough. Yes, I hate women too and agree that one Mass is more terrible to me than 10,000 armed invaders. Please charge me what you like and send me the **John Knox Collectible Bear**.
Name _____
Address of secure wing in Liff /Royal Edinburgh/Carstairs (delete as appropriate)
_____

☐ Join our mailing list
Yes, there's more tat on the way

*Legal Disclaimer: Runaway Success in this instance could, strictly speaking, be interpreted to mean that we had so many of them left that we stuck grey beards on them and thought up this ad as a way to shift a couple of dozen more.

Celebrity **AGONY** Column

The Agony Column with real Agony!

Dear Mr Knox
I've been married for seven years now and although I love my husband I don't fancy him any more. I've met this really nice man where I work. He's the opposite of my husband. He's very sexy and when he kisses me I almost explode with joy. We've been to bed a couple of times and it was wonderful. My problem is do you think I should leave my husband for this man and all the pleasure he offers or stay with my marriage and the financial security that it offers.
Yours, Unsure

Dear Unsure
YOU ADULTEROUS FORNICATOR!!!! I WILL BE ROUND, SHORTLY, TO WHIP YOU WITHIN AN INCH OF YOUR LIFE!!! GOD IS VERY VERY ANGRY WITH YOU!!! YOU FOR ONE WON'T BE GETTING A TICKET FOR A NEVER-ENDING AFTERLIFE!!! DO NOT WRITE AGAIN AND FURTHER SOIL MY LETTER BOX WITH YOUR FILTH!!!!!
Yours sincerely, John Knox

Dear Mr Knox
Does God love Pickles, my hamster. My Daddy says that when Pickles dies he'll go to straight to heaven. But I want to make sure.
Tracy Tuppence
P.S. Daddy says that he hopes that

Tommy Hamilton goes to heaven too, even though he shouldn't be using that bit of land.

Dear Tracy
NO! GOD DOESN'T WANT HAMSTERS IN HEAVEN. IS PICKLES ONE OF THE CHOSEN? I THINK NOT!!! ENJOY HIS COMPANY WHILE YOU CAN!!!
Best regards, John Knox
**P.S. YOU WON'T BE GOING EITHER UNLESS YOU MEND YOUR WAYS!!!
P.P.S. YES TOMMY WILL BE GOING TO HEAVEN. HE'S BEEN CHOSEN. TOUGH BUT THERE IT IS!!!**

Dear Mr Knox
Sometimes I am tempted to write rude things about monks on the friary walls. Can you help me?
Confused

Dear Confused
WRITING RUDE THINGS?? GOD IS VERY ANGRY WITH YOU AND YOUR LACK OF AMBITION!!! YOU SHOULD BE BURNING DOWN THESE BUILDINGS, TRASHING IDOLATROUS IMAGES, HARASSING THIEVING FRIARS AND THROWING THEM OUT OF SCOTLAND!!!! IT IS THE CHRISTIAN WAY!!!
Best, John Knox

Advertorial

The Scottish Presbyterian Friendly Society.
A letter from our chairman, Mr John Knox

Dear Friends

I know a lot of you will get this circular and your first thought will be to crumple it up and throw it in the bin. But wait! Just hold your garrons a moment! All we are asking is that you give us just a couple of minutes of your time and then maybe we can make some big savings for you.

Savings? What does he mean? Is he offering to save our souls? He can't guarantee eternal paradise, can he? When I shuffle off this mortal coil can he book me a pew in heaven?'

I know you're all thinking these questions to yourselves and more. 'How can that nice Mr Knox promise an eternally pleasurable afterlife?' And no doubt you'll add: 'I'd like my soul to be one of those in the first class carriage, but how?'

The answer is that it's not easy. But then nothing worthwhile is easy, is it? What does he know you might rightly ask? You've seen me swanning about Edinburgh, living the easy life, a bit of preaching, a nice salary so I can give the kids a good education. But I learnt the hard way. Nineteen months as a galley slave. Trained as a preacher and a lawyer what did I know about rowing a ship? That's right, a big fat nothing! It was hard on my physical body but God stood by me and at the end, He said to me: 'John my boy, you've earned your ticket. Now off you go and save some souls for me.'

So what do you think now? Come along to St Giles. I'll be signing copies of my books and saving a few souls, so you might get lucky.

Yours

John.

Dear Ms Elizabeth the First
I enclose my application for stand-in Queen.
If there is any further information that you
need, please do not hesitate to send a man on
a horse.
Yours Sincerely

Mary, Queen of Scots

Application

I would like to apply for the post of stand-
in Queen. I am prepared to hang around to
provide that necessary queenly waving, now
considered an essential part of the modern
royal pageant, when you need to pop off to
powder your nose, or indeed the rest of your
face.

Perhaps you will need a couple of days off.
You might be interested in a mini- break in
Spain or to the Royal Parks. I could fill in
for you and repress peasants, execute unruly
nobles who have got too big for their
breeches, and ensure that the court remains a
gay elegant place. I could even do a bit of
minor ruling, if need be.

I have a lot of experience in being a queen,
and have successfully ruled a small country
for a number years. Having parted amicably
from my previous employer, I am currently
between kingdoms. I have many skills,
including man-management, languages, hunting,
riding, and I come equipped with my own wig.

Should I be successful, I would require every
Sunday off and all Saints' feast days available to be spent in religious contemplation.

New Year's Resolutions

James VI
■ 'This year I'm going to give up court favourites. I know I say it every year but this time I mean it. It started out with just one or two at a time – but now I'm up to 40 a day. It's beyond a joke.'

Mary, Queen of Scots
■ 'I'm giving up the Mass. It's time I turned aside from the accursed church of Rome – the 'synagogue of Satan' as my good friend John Knox puts it. Ho, ho, ho! Only joking.'

James V (turning his head to the wall after defeat at Solway Moss)
■ 'I'm just giving up.'

Sons and Mothers

There wasn't really much chance for maternal bonding between James, the future king of Scotland and England, and Mary, Queen of Scots.

She was forced to abdicate, partly on the insistence of her cousin Lord James Stewart, Earl of Moray, and partly because even in Stewart terms she was a pretty unsuccessful monarch. Which in itself was an achievement, as her predecessors had set particularly low standards.

Mary went into exile in England after losing the battle of Langside. She was something of an embarrassment and was shuffled round England for 18 years at the behest of another cousin, Elizabeth, Queen of England. Mary's son was stuck in Scotland getting a very unsatisfactory and one-sided education from George Buchanan.

Until the death of Darnley, Buchanan had been unswervingly loyal to Mary. However, this brutal murder changed his mind about her and from that moment on he became completely and fiercely opposed to the Queen. One of the manifestations of this occurred when he took it upon himself to educate the young James. Along with a rigid protestant didactic, lessons also poisoned his mind against his mother.

When Mary was executed, James did feel that it was a personal slight to him. However, as she was a potential barrier to his ultimate ambition, he didn't kick up much of a fuss. He wanted to be king of England above everything else.

Name Shame Heartache of Star Trek Actor

Star Trek actor Patrick Stewart yesterday spoke about his heartache over his namesake, Patrick Stewart, Earl of Orkney. 'I can't tell you how many times I've had to explain that I'm not the same man!' he told us by phone from LA. 'And despite the many time-travel plots we used in Star Trek, I've never even been to the 16th Century.'

The controversial Patrick, Earl of Orkney, was known for his ruthless treatment of friends and foes alike. On succeeding his father, the equally callous Robert, in 1593, he continued his father's tradition of ruling the Orcadians with an iron fist. His estate was tended by slave labour culled from the downtrodden tenants. Some commentators have pointed out that he did create one of the most gracious Renaissance buildings in Scotland, the Earl's Palace at Kirkwall. But his 21st-century actor namesake is not one to mince words. 'The man was a despot,' he commented in those famous Shakespearian tones. 'It's no joke sharing a name with someone whose name is a byword for tyranny and exploitation of his tenants. It's jolly embarrassing, I can tell you.'

A King of the People

It's a real scoop, the first interview with the James VI, the new King. In 1603 he became King of Scotland and England. We all now have a chance to find out what it been like, and he came across as a well-balanced and concerned modern king.

'Well, you know, anyone could have been King,' he claimed modestly, 'I just happened to be the right person with royal blood in his veins in the right place at the right time. But, do you know, now that I am King I want to make sure that justice prevails, that the poor are treated equally with the rich. I'd really like to alleviate the suffering of my people.'

Brave sentiments from a brave man. While we chatted to him, some of his advisors came past.

The Duke of Buckingham, a fine-looking man, engaged us on the subject of ruffs.

The King had finished signing a few papers telling the Scots what to do, so we asked him about the nasty Ruthvens and the Gowrie Conspiracy. A sign of his greatness was the way he regretted the bloodshed. 'We should always be able to talk about our problems. But when John Ruthven, Earl of Gowrie, and his brother the Master of Ruthven, laid their hands on my person there was nothing I could do to stop my loyal courtiers from striking out. We were very sad that they both died with loads of stab wounds and I had to take all their family's lands and property, and even proscribe their name. A terrible shame.'

Own Your Own

Ghost in a Bottle

Scotland's castles are synonymous with ghosts. Green ladies, grey ladies, even black ladies. Have you ever wished your house could have a ghost of its own?

Well now it can! Just send off for the Scots Wha Hae

Ghost in a Bottle

It may look like an empty bottle with a label on it. But it contains a 100% genuine Scottish ghost, as found in castles like Glamis, and other strongholds like that.

Here are just some of the strange phenomena you will experience:

- Ballpoint pens mysteriously vanish into thin air
- Put two socks into the wash – take just one out
- Your bin seems to fill with rubbish all by itself
- Missing objects move them-selves to the last place you look
- You can find every newspaper for the last three weeks, except today's
- The toilet seat is never in the position you last left it

'I bought a Scots Wha Hae Bottled Ghost and now I'm hooked. I have Mac von Sydow coming round later to observe the incredible things happening to me.'
Diana J Weinstein III

How to be King by **James I and VI**

Oh la, I'm so weary today. I've been up since 11.30, ruling. It's such a tiresome job. Thank God, I'm having an early lunch.

So how do you become king? Dear friends, there are many ways. I, myself, was chosen by God, personally. Some of the English kings use a mystical experience to give their rule validity: a magical sword drawn from a stone. There are some countries where the nobles just fight each other and the strongest becomes king. But that really is very working class and they never get invited to the top-notch weddings or get to make alliances with genuine kings, like myself. One of the good things about being chosen by God is that if we ever have to go into battle, He'll be on our side so we always win.

So what does a king do then? Some people think we just lie around all the day and only rise to eat. Ha, ha, ha, that couldn't be further from the truth. I have to work long hours and the days are so full, writing poetry, choosing clothes – did you know that I'm expected to seduce loads of people? Then there are the official functions, it's an endless stream of 20-course banquets with half-naked serving wenches and all the wine you can drink. As you can see, it's a job like everyone else's – it's just a bit more white collar than being a lobster potter.

TV Guide Pick of the Day

2.0 **Dynasty**
Those Stewarts are at it again. James I and VI is long buried, and his successor Charles I has steered the family business to ruin, and finally loses his head. A rival firm, Roundhead Inc, have managed a corporate takeover, led by the despicable CEO, Oliver Cromwell. Despite valiant opposition by Charles's area manager, the Marquis of Montrose, his rights issue never takes off, and soon Montrose is removed. All seems lost for Stewart Holdings – but Cromwell is getting old, and can Charles II save the day? It is looking rosier for the Stewarts, but the business could soon pass to Charles's brother, James VII, and a Dutch competitor could still sink the battling Stewarts.

3.30 **Christmas Message from Oliver Cromwell**
Oliver Cromwell spreads the festive cheer by banning Christmas, dancing, and singing. It's not all bad news, though: our glorious Lord Protector has confirmed the abolition of tax on warts.

Weight Problems?
Clothes Won't Fit?

Want to Lose *THAT* Ugly Fat?

Now you can with the S-plan diet

'I lost six stone in two weeks.'
Alexander Ramsay of Dalhousie
'I am just skin and bone.'
David Stewart, Duke of Rothesay
'I'm as thin as a wraith.'
Dunty Porteous the Miller

It could not be more easy. Simply get locked up in a dungeon in the castle of your choice and have them throw away the key. Available at our health spas at Hermitage, Falkland, and Spedlins – and throughout Scotland.

With S-plan weight loss is easy.

Or why not try our alternative S-B (salted-beef) diet? Simply eat lots of very salted beef. And then get locked up in a dungeon in the castle of your choice and have them throw away the key. And make sure you have no water. At all.

'I can only rave about this diet. Now leave me alone while I gnaw the door.'
Hugh MacDonald
'You would be mad not to use the S-B diet.'
John Sinclair, Master of Caithness

Only available at our health spas at Duntulm and Girnigoe.

With S-B plan weight loss is easy.

The Best of Times ...
Dirk Y. Looter

It's about this time in the year, during a really bloody civil war, that the keen scavenger tends to find a nice fresh fall of breastplates, halberds and helmets. You'll often find them with their big bags and a patient pony collecting up the detritus of war. It's a thankless task, apart from loads of money. But they wouldn't have it any other way.

'When I was a young lad, I used to tag along with my Dad. He used to be a camp follower: he'd dragged himself out of the gutter. He'd joined up when he saw the ads. Travel the length and breadth of Britain, they said. He's been all over the place: Naseby, Marston Moor, Philiphaugh, Dunbar, Inverkeithing. You know he even did one foreign trip. He said it was quite interesting, but the fancy French food didn't agree with him.

'I'm a bit more of a homebody, but there has been plenty here to keep me and the bairns in life's little luxuries. We have a roof over our heads, which the neighbours are very jealous of, and fresh straw on the beds once a month.

'But it is not an easy life – there is a lot of carrying you have to do. We like to get onto the battlefield soon after the fighting has died down. When the corpses are still warm, it's easier to get the armour off them. They stiffen up pretty quickly. You have to be quite canny though, because every now and then you come across a live one. The rules are strict and you can only plunder the dead: so I carry this large handy knife with me.

'The fashions have fair changed since I was a lad and of course you don't get so many of the nobility dead. They tend to direct things from the back nowadays. My dad told me that his great-great-great grandfather had even came across a King. He said it was a James but then I suppose that is what they were all called in those days.'

Montrose to Head New Decorative Scheme

The authorities in Edinburgh today announced that James Graham, Marquis of Montrose, was going to be the leading figure in the city's new summer show.

'We feel that someone of his stature would be the ideal choice. Everyone has heard of him and the youngsters go mad for him.'

Some critics accused the city fathers of dumbing down. 'There was a time when it was priests and intellectuals who were given pride of place. Now it is just some coarse soldier.'

Many priests and intellectuals, however, are privately pleased that it is the Earl's head that is to be stuck on a spike on the city wall.

It certainly is an improvement from their point of view.

The Best of Times ...
Archbishop Sharp

I had a bit of a scare the other day. This young lad set off a firearm near me. Gave me a bit of a start. I imagine it was a gang of rowdy loons celebrating some sporting success. It does give you a bit of a turn, but I'm not worried because the people have a great deal of affection for me.

Life has been good, and now I feel much more centred. You know, I had a bit of a rough time down in London. I think I'd been a bit vocal in my support for the Crown when Oliver Cromwell was about. You know he could be a bit touchy about that. He was a bit touchy about pretty much everything: the monarchy, the church, parliament, his warts. Best to avoid most subjects at the dinner table and stick to safe topics, like raising sheep or best of all – I find – is just to praise God a lot. You know, 'thank you God for that Brussels Sprout'.

Anyway, we got over our little tiff and soon I was back in the saddle doing a bit of negotiating. When Charles II was restored – ha ha, makes him sound like a bit of furniture, doesn't it? Anyway, when Charles II came back, I was well rewarded by being made Archbishop of Scotland.

I've heard the rumours and, yes: I can be tough; but it is a caring toughness. You can't make an omelette without breaking a few eggs. I've heard some rather spoilt people say I'm harsh – but that's so unfair. You can ask anyone about how sensitive I am. I think a lot of people don't really realise the strain of being an Archbishop. I've not just got to write all my sermons and take all those services, but I've also got to save people's souls. It takes a lot of energy.

It's also really unfair that people complain about money. Yes, even I have had that 'fat cat' epithet hurled at me. I'm not embarrassed about my wealth; I believe that I've earned it. Yes, I have a nice house in Fife, my tailor is really very good, and I've got the most up-to-date carriage money can buy, but, do you know, I've worked for them.

When I want to relax after a hard day performing the King's and God's work I like to get out in the fresh air. Actually, I'm going for a little jaunt round Magus Moor with my daughter next week. We've got some new extra comfy cushions to die for, and I'd like to try them out.

How to Scratch a Living by **Grubby MacKenzie**

In our continuing series, we had the good luck to run into a dirt-poor peasant who, for a share of some peapods and half a turnip, is going to give us some insight into living on the poverty line.

'Aye, every day's long and hard and very poorly rewarded. If you want to survive you need to spend all day digging for roots or collecting wind-fall fruit. It's best that you have no education and little native wit. If you had either of those you'd soon realise that you're fighting a losing battle and give up.'

But you're your own man!

'No. The chieftain owns us and we have to do everything he says, however daft. It's a bloody awful life, cold and wet. Our clothes are all rags, hairy and uncomfortable at the best of times. Our hovels let the rain in. The mud gets everywhere. The worst of it is the tourists come round to look at as us as if we were some African savages. I'd swap places with them any time, at least they can get warm.

'If you want to scratch a living, then you can't do any worse than here. Winter or Summer, the Highlands have nothing to make life pleasant.'

What about the beautiful countryside?

'You must be from another planet.

'Anyway, I'm forgetting my manners: can I offer you a handful of dirt and some ditchwater?'

Top Nobles To Form Union

Some of the top figures in England and Scotland have decided to form a new Union. They say that it would be far easier to ensure that money is divided fairly between England and Scotland.

We challenged their spokesman that our nobles were, in fact, trying to grab as much cash as possible. He explained that being a noble entailed far more expenditure than the ordinary person, and therefore it was only equitable that they receive a higher percentage.

He got very huffy when we suggested they were just grabbing as much as they could for themselves.

'I've had enough of these innuendoes and slurs: talk plainly. What are you trying to say? Just come out with it for goodness's sake, speak your mind.'

'You're just nicking all our money!!'

'The trouble with you reporters is that you just can't bring yourselves to ask questions without wrapping them up in verbiage. Nobody knows what you mean. I can't be bothered to decipher this strange code. We nobles are just going to go off and do our best for Scotland, as usual, despite your negativity.'

So there we have it. They're going to run roughshod over the ordinary Scot again, as they have done for the last few hundred years. But this time they sold us out to the English too!

Scottish Journeys

I never thought much of that General Wade. And I'm not sure I agreed with the sentiments of the National Anthem that he should, 'confound our policies and frustrate our knavish tricks', that's not very neighbourly is it? But you have to hand it to the man: those roads are a big improvement. I can get in my carriage and it's just a hop and a skip from Fort Augustus to Drumnadrochit. Of course it means the wife's mother can pop down whenever she wants. But every cloud has a silver lining. They say he's built 240 miles of road and 40 bridges. He always seemed such a little man, but there's no telling with some people.

TV Guide

7.45 Dynasty
Those Stewarts are at it again. James VII did a runner when the Dutch conglomerate, Orange Enterprises, muscled in on the Stewarts' markets. Family squabbles followed when it was found that the takeover was being masterminded by James's plain daughter, Mary, who married William, CEO of Orange Enterprises. When William dies mysteriously, it is left to the Stewarts to attempt to restore their fortunes. However, when Anne, another daughter of James, seizes control it can only mean trouble for James VII, and his son and heir, another James, just to confuse things. Despite corporate manoeuvring, involving many multinationals, it looks like curtains for the Stewarts when the German House of Hanover makes a decisive bid for all of the Stewarts' assets.

9.0 Your Money or Your Life
Scotland has severe money worries. What would you do? Save your Scottish pounds and act prudently, or throw all your money into a hair-brained scheme to found a colony on Panama?

9.30 Food and Drink
The Earl of Argyll features in tonight's show, and explains how to get a really good smoky flavour from flame-grilled MacDonalds.

9.30 Holiday Show
Hannah Gordon tours the north and visits Glencoe with Robert Campbell of Glenlyon, looking for some real Highland hospitality.

10.0 Star Trek: The Next Generation
A temporal anomaly casts Captain Picard back to 16th-century Orkney, where he must face his nemesis, Earl Patrick Stewart.

Know Your Jameses!

James I came to the throne when he was 29. He spent the first years driving about in his four-wheel off-roader and comparing the prices of castles with his nobles. He ordered that building patios should be compulsory.

James II came to the throne when he was six. He decreed that Pokemón cards be made legal tender and made noodle doodles and fish fingers a regular feature of Royal banquets. He drank nothing but fizzy juice.

James III came to the throne when he was eight. He revolutionised warfare by making nipping, scratching and Chinese burns the only legitimate weapons of war. In addition, he extended his influence to the education system by banning all homework.

James IV came to the throne when he was 15. His first act was to paint the inside of his castle black. He then spent the first year of his reign playing on the Internet and listening to heavy metal music.

James V was one year old when he came to the throne. His policies included kicking his legs in the air, dribbling, and sleeping one hour out of every two.

James VI became king when he was 14 but there was no time for any teenage king japes as he was kidnapped and held at Ruthven Castle for several years.

James VII became king when he was 52. He abolished tax on joint embrocation, and encouraged moralising about the 'good old days'. He forced his subjects to drink endless cups of tea.

James VIII never became king at all.

The Bonnie Prince Charlie Letters

Dear Dad

I've landed in Scotland as you told me to. It is quite backward here. The people are a bit rough spoken. Actually they're very rough. We're staying in a Bed-and-Breakfast in Ardnamurchan. The bed is a bit crowded since there are the seven of us who landed at Moidart and John O'Sullivan has brought a pig. I'd never had porridge before so I said I'd try it but to be honest I don't want to try it ever again. I'm beginning to wonder why I left France. Getting a taste for the whisky, though.

Love to you and my bro. Harry

Charles

Dear Dad

I've met a very nice man called Donald Cameron. It is very odd since he also seems to be called Lochiel. Can't they just settle on one name and stick to it? He has a rather odd habit of calling me Bonnie. It rather sounds like he's calling his labrador. Anyway he introduced me to Clanranald. At first I thought we were going to meet a whole clan but it just turned out to be one person. Anyway after a lot of chat they've agreed to come along. We're going to Prestonpans. It really doesn't sound very romantic but I suppose we have to go somewhere because there is a dearth of decent restaurants here in the Highlands. There is apparently a very good fish and chip shop there. What does that mean?

Yours, Charlie

P.S. One of the rough looking soldiers came into my tent while I was

The Bonnie Prince Charlie Letters

polishing my medal from Gaeta. Apparently we've just won a battle. Well that's a good bit of news. I must be a better general than I thought. Aren't you pleased with me?

Hello there Pater

We've spent a very pleasant winter in Edinburgh. It is a bit of a smelly city but apart from that it's not such a bad place to stay in for a couple of months. I think we're all going to go down to London now. My friends say I'll really enjoy it down there as it's a bit more sophisticated than Scotland. Between you and me, I find them all a bit backward, even in the capital. You should see how old fashioned their wigs are and the ruffs just don't bear talking about.

Charlie

Hi there Daddy

We've got into a bit of trouble. We were on our way to London and this big bully called Mr Cumberland started looking for trouble. He's a butcher apparently. We're having to head back north pronto. Actually I don't like it any more. Although have made a new friend called Clementina. She has shown me a new game called 'Hide the Haggis', which I have come to enjoy. But I want to come home. Everyone wants to go to Culloden so I'll go up there with them but then I'm coming back home.

Hope to see you very soon

All my love, Charlie

Demands for War Crimes Trial Grows

More news reports are coming in of atrocities committed after the Battle of Culloden. At the battle on 16 April, the Jacobite army of Charles Edward Stewart, mostly made up of Highlanders, was defeated by government forces led by the Duke of Cumberland, son of George II. The Duke has been lavished with praise by both Houses of Parliament and given an extra £25 000 a year.

Although the Jacobites had rebelled against our rightful king, their army had generally behaved well on its travels, avoiding looting, pillage, murder and rapine. **The same cannot be said of our troops.**

We can reveal that after the Battle of Culloden:
- Maimed Jacobites were **MURDERED** where they lay
- Nineteen wounded Jacobite officers were **SUMMARILY EXECUTED** at Culloden House by being shot and then **BLUDGEONED TO DEATH** with musket butts
- Forty Highlanders were **BURNED ALIVE** in a thatched cottage, despite trying to surrender
- Ordinary citizens in the surrounding area were **MASSACRED**, mistaken for Jacobites
- government soldiery **BEDAUBED EACH OTHER WITH BLOOD**

Have Cumberland and the government forces gone too far? Many feel the actions of government forces amount to war crimes, and these should be properly investigated. We live in the 18th century, and barbarism should not be tolerated by anyone.

Government sources have claimed that the Jacobites had orders to refuse quarter to government forces, but we now know that this was a complete fabrication. The Duke of Cumberland has been reported as saying that the Jacobites, having risen in rebellion against his father, were 'not entitled to the rights of humanity'.

Further action is believed to be about to be taken against Highlanders, such as the banning of weapons, driving off of stock and burning of houses, the proscription of Highland dress, bagpipes, the tearing down of the whole clan system, and the building of forts.

Is it not time we actually addressed the grievances of those who live in the Highlands, such as poverty, disease, and hunger?

ESSENTIAL GUIDE TO

Keicha

one of the most scenic parts of Scotland

Why not plan your visit today?

You will already have heard something about the fascinating heritage, the wonderful environment, the stunning outdoor activities on Keicha. To help you navigate around Keicha, the following guide lists all the best places to visit and see.

INVERARGH AREA

Inverargh is a plain old town of white-washed buildings, dating from about 1784. It was moved to its present location by the MacCams of Inverargh at the end of the 18th century as they wanted the peasants moved from near their castle to make way for pheasants and sheep.

Inverargh Castle

1 mile N of Inverargh.
Family home of the famous MacCam clan. The present castle was completed in 1754 and resembles a power station. The old picturesque castle was then ironically demolished as an eyesore.

The castle is simply crammed with family portraits, and there is a clan room with more family portraits. One item of interest is the underwear soiled by Bonnie Prince Charlie at the Battle of Culloden. And more family portraits.

The MacCams came to prominence in the 14th century. The clan slogan is 'Argh', the sound made by their enemies, mostly women and children, as they burned in their homes. The clan were made Dukes of Keicha after the Union of Parliaments in 1707, and a large bribe. The family rewarded the loyalty of their clansmen by clearing them and replacing them with sheep. This is why so many clansmen now live anywhere but Scotland. The MacCam male line died out in 1825: the family name is actually MacCam-Douglas-Winstanley-Woddrop-Primrose-Plantaganet.
Explanatory displays. Guided tours all the time: so you will be sandwiched between coach parties and not see the family portraits even

if you wanted to. Gift shop with MacCam souvenirs. Cafe in servant's kitchen: where else? WC. Disabled access as long as they have entrance fee. Gardens not open to public. Coach and car parking. £7.50 per head and count yourself lucky. And did we mention the family portraits.
Open 21 Apr-29 Oct, Mon-Thu 10.00-17.00, Fri 11.00-12.30, Sat 8.30-17.30, Sun 12.32-14.44; closed Bank Hols and some Mon and Fri; Tue in Jul.

Inverargh Institute Museum
High Street, Inverargh.
The museum has displays on the history of the town, including Neolithic pottery, stuffed birds, old school photographs, lavatory bowls and communion tokens, as well as an archive on local families. It could be really interesting if the institute was given resources to update their exhibition, catalogue their archive, and maybe get a wee gift shop and a cafe. Run by volunteers with no grants from anyone.
Explanatory displays. No facilities. No disabled access. Parking nearby. FREE.
Open mid Jun-mid Aug, Thu 13.00-17.00, Fri 9.30-17.00, Sat-Sun 13.00-17.00 - or when volunteers can get time.

The Big Moonshine
White Elephant Road, Inverargh.
New, fascinating attraction, housed in a custom-built dome costing millions of pounds. It combines all the latest computer techniques and interactive technology to provide the visitor with an unforgettable experience. There are hands-on activities for children, giant television walls, audioguide, holographic displays and digital tour guides. Completely funded by money from the National Lottery, European Social Fund, local government and grants from just about everybody.
Amazing experience for the visitor. Gift shops. Cafe and restaurant. Sports facilities. Swimming pool. Full disabled access. Car and coach parking. £5.50 per head.
Open all year: daily 9.00-21.00; closed 25 Dec.

Glen Gormless Distillery
Glen Gormless, 3 miles SE of Inverargh.
The distillery was founded in 1964 and is an ugly building, which resembles Inverargh Castle. Produced here is the famous Old Gormless Single Malt Whisky, which has a peaty full flavour, with just a hint of sewerage. Water comes from the Stinky Burn. Most of the whisky produced at Glen Gormless goes to blended whisky, while the rest is used to clean out the cylinders of car engines and etch titanium. A tour of the distillery is available, and there is an exhibition 'Turning Barley, Malt

and Water into Gold: Who Gets Filthy Rich from Malt Whisky'. Children under eight are not allowed in the production areas which is as well as the little buggers would be bored stupid. Visitors receive a free dram: try driving after drinking that on an empty stomach.

Explanatory displays. Visitor centre. Gift shop. WC. Disabled access to visitor centre. Car and coach parking. £3.50 per head.

Open all year: Mon-Fri 9.30-17.00.

St Bhartean's Pictish Stones Museum

7.5 miles SW of Invergargh.

The excellent museum houses some of the best examples of Dark Age sculpture in the whole of Europe. St Bhartean's Stone has scenes of hunters, beasts and symbols, all carved expertly in high relief, as well as an Ogham inscription which reads 'Now Wash Your Hands'. There are 23 other fragments of carved stones and crosses.

Explanatory displays. Parking nearby.

Open? Actually inexplicably closed for years.

St Bhartean's Church

St Bhartean's, 7.5 miles SW of Invergargh.

Standing on a large mound, this is a fine rectangular church, dating from the 15th century, with part of the original rood screen, large medieval paintings, alms dish and sacrament house. This is one of the best preserved medieval churches in Scotland.

Open: get key from nearby house (if they are in, which they never are)

CLUDGE TOWN AREA

Cludge was once an industrial power house, and its domestic products were used in virtually every part of the world. Cludge has seen some harder times recently, but it now going through a period of renovation and growth, particularly in violence, poverty, alcoholism and drug taking.

Porcelain Works

Sewerage Lane, Cludge

Opened in 2000, this is a major museum and heritage centre which charts the rise of Cludge from a small fishing village to one of the powerhouses of Industrial Revolution Britain. It was here, in a restored factory, that the famous Cludge toilet bowls were manufactured. There are breathtaking displays, using sights, sounds and smells, on the manufacture of toilet bowls from raw materials to finished product, a restored worker's cottage of 1910, and an audio-visual show depicting the story of Cludge from earliest times. An interactive experience allows the visitor to drive a local commuter train on a recreation of the former railway line, dodging bricks thrown from bridges and concrete blocks laid on the track.

Explanatory displays. Audio-visual presentations. Gift shop. Cafe. Disabled access. Car and coach parking. FREE.

Open all year, daily 9.00-17.00.
*** Please note that due to a recent arson attack, the museum will be closed for the foreseeable future. ***

Cludge Castle
On coast, Cludge Town.

Formerly a picturesque ruin, perched high on cliffs. Unfortunately, it has all crumbled into the sea due to years of vandalisation and disinterest by the local authority. A plaque does mark the spot, although this was defaced by Wee Malkie and now bears a comic phallus.

Cludge Castle was held by the MacLavies, enemies of the MacCams of Inverargh. Their rivalry came to a head at the Battle of Bottom Bay. The chief of the MacLavies was in the privy, and the MacCams set it on fire, killing him. The rest of the clan went down the pan.

Explanatory plaque. Empty beer cans and used condoms. Broken bottles. Ugly youths with flick knives.

Access at all reasonable times.

Haggis Stone
Cludge Beach

This hilariously shaped rock is hilariously shaped like a haggis. To the uninitiated, it can look like many other hilarious haggis-shaped stones, but the locals can point it out if they are not too out of their heads on glue.

Access at all reasonable times.

Old Cludge Rare Breed Farm and Organic Tannery
One mile north of Cludge.

Something for everyone in your family, and a popular day out. The farm has many rare breeds of sheep and pigs, as well as other domestic animals. In the children's farm, many of the sweet young furry animals can be fed and petted. In the slaughterhouse, you can watch older animals being killed and skinned. In the tannery you can view the various processes of tanning hides, from gore-splattered skin to finished product. In our restaurant you can eat what is left, and in our shop purchase the skins and take home a bit of animal, yours to own forever.

Visitor centre. Gift shop selling hides. Restaurant serving the most succulent cuts of Bambi, Thumper, Ermintrude, Flossie and Babe. Car and coach parking. FREE.

Open all year, daily 9.00-17.00.

WINDDALE AREA

This is the most picturesque part of Keicha. The land rises from the sea to wooded hills and then into the higher grounds and purple mountains of Reekie. Winddale village stands by a bay and was once a centre for slate quarrying, while Reekie has always been agricultural and is a haven for wildlife and walkers.

MacTat's Tartan Trash

Winddale, 7 miles W of Garbay.

Simply stuffed with unbelievable items, such as a lavatory seat which plays 'Flower of Scotland' and 'Charlie is My Darling', astounding poems and shocking paintings by A. B. C. MacTat, tartan- and kilt-clad dolls of Mary Queen of Scots, and the William Wallace Heirloom Collectible Bear. Winddale is actually a very interesting place: the small island of Papa Winddale has a fascinating museum, old slate quarries, a picturesque walk, and a friendly pub which serves excellent seafood: all the best of Scotland on one small island. Alas, coach parties taken to Winddale only have time to see around MacTat's Tartan Trash before being herded back onto the bus.

Unique gift shop. Coach and coach parking. Fascinating island of Papa Winddale two minute ferry ride away but for some reason everyone goes to MacTat's Tartan Trash Shop instead. Strange old world.

Open Apr-Sep, 9.00-17.00.

Winddale Sea Adventure Tours

Winddale.

With Sea Adventure Tours you can visit the famous tumultuous waters of the Corriesplooshing whirlpool. The tours are in fully accredited rubber dinghies with all the latest safety equipment and are helmed by experienced mariners who know the waters like the back of their hand and wear oil skins and have big black sailor's beards. The fact that none of the locals would dream of going on the boats has nothing at all to do with the fact that several times the outboards have failed and the boat came within a hair of being sucked into the whirlpool or that time when that child fell overboard and was nearly drowned or that time an easterly blew up and the boat got swamped by a giant wave. After all, nobody has been drowned - yet. So hang on for dear life: this is excitement which cannot be matched!

Tours of whirlpool and islands. All boats have direct link with coastguard. Sea Rescue Helicopter trip home certain days (no extra charge). £11.50 per head.

Open all year: daily 9.00-17.00; tours every hour, except if all drowned.

Mid Reekie Chambered Cairn
Four miles S of Garbay.

The chambered cairn is one of the best Neolithic monuments on Keicha, and stands on farm land, about 0.5 miles from the main road. The chamber is still covered, and a 30 foot passageway leads to a central chamber with three side cells. The bones of 34 individuals were found here. Visitors may be fooled by the 'Keep Out' sign left the by local farmer, as well as the 'Beware of the Bull'. These should not be taken seriously: bulls rarely kill anyone, as fans of Spanish bullfighting will testify. The fact that the farmer keeps lurking about with a shotgun to make sure you are not worrying his sheep should also not prevent you from fully enjoying your visit. Then there is the cunningly placed barbed wire, and the pack of rabid sheep dogs.

Access at all reasonable times if you are Indiana Jones.

Clan English Centre, Over Reekie
Over Reekie, 3 miles south of Garbay.

This is the clan centre for the English, for all those from south of the border with no Scottish or Irish connection. Here you can find out all about your clan heritage: which tartan you would have worn had the English had clans and what you might have got up to if you were not English. Then nip off to the adjacent tartan shop to purchase your clan tartan, kilts, sporrans, cap badges, haggis, whisky, dirks, Lochaber axes, chip butties, birlinns and garrons. Everything for you, the English person, to make a clan out of your family! Also visit our Clan Antarctica Centre, Clan South America Centre, and Clan Turkmanistan Centre.

Explanatory displays. Tartan gift shop. Cafe serving traditional Scottish food: deep fried. Car and coach parking. £3 per head.

Open all year: daily 9.00-17.00; closed 1-10 Jan to recover from Hogmanay spent in Brighton.

Roman Signal Station, Under Reekie
Five miles south of Garbay.

One of a chain of Roman signal stations, built to warn of invasion by northern tribes. There are said to be earthworks, and if you find a slight indentation in the ground interesting, then this is for you. Luckily the site is signposted otherwise you would never find it.

Access at all reasonable times.

Issued by the Keicha Tourist Board, er no, visitkeicha, Visitkeicha, or VisitKeicha? Something like that. Anyway, who cares? We're off to the sunny beaches of Ibiza to get plastered, sunburnt and laid.

Kilts Banned!

There was uproar when the latest restriction on the true Scot became known. The English have banned the kilt in the Disclothing Act! It was retaliation for the cheerful carnival that Prince Charlie organised to cheer up some of the glummer folk on the other side of the border in 1745 and 46. Typically, the sour-faced members of parliament have passed a bill outlawing the wearing of the kilt – except in the army.

The Bonnie Prince was just trying to liven things up a little. Give folk something to take their minds off work. Everyone likes a nice little war. It gets the blood going and, of course, new opportunities can open up when your boss is a victim of the random slaughter.

Anyway, there is still hope for us kilt lovers everywhere. I, for one, still have a rash from my own tartan garment. The influential Guild of Humorists and Stand-up Comedians have been one of the first groups to demand that the restrictions be lifted.

'It immediately and irreparably damages some of this country's finest hilarious moments,' a spokesman said. 'Fundamental jokes as the classic, "is anything worn under the kilt?" no longer have the impact they used to have.' He added: 'We want them off. The restrictions that is. They should be lifted, the bans I mean. Let's strip them all away and run naked in the hills, er, sorry, sorry I was just thinking of something else then.'

Thank you. So with the Guild on our side it can't be long before we'll be out of our trousers and the air can freely circulate once again around our vital organs.

Gow-A-Bunga

What a star! Just watch those chubby little fingers go. Not only is Neil Gow the fiddler's fiddler, but he has that rare gift of appealing to the young bucks and their sweethearts as well. Listening to his latest tunes makes your heart skip and your feet tap. But don't just take it from me. The Duke of Atholl is a big fan too.

'Your Grace, Neil Gow, best fiddler in the world?'

'I'd say so: I've patronised him for some years now.'

'I thought you patronised everyone?'

'In this case, I actually gave him money. He just gets better and better. You know, I may be an old fuddy-duddy but I like to hear proper music. A song with a melody and not your modern tuneless dance music such as they play on the Highland pipes. Gow's music certainly helped take my mind off things when in 1746 my perfidious brother Lord George Murray was besieging Blair Castle.'

'You didn't get on, then?'

'Just a little sibling rivalry. Plus the fact that we'd ended up on opposite sides in the 1745 uprising. We managed to patch things up and my daughter married his son. A nice little bit of business that reunited the family properties.'

'Anyway if you can't get to see him in the flesh, go and have a look at the portrait by Raeburn and you can almost imagine him fiddling away. Neil Gow I mean.'

An Ewe Day Dawns
Advertorial on behalf of the Sheep Marketing Board.

1760 and it is time to salute the new invention by Robert Bakewell: the Cheviot Sheep! He says, 'It's the best sheep in the world'. If you're looking to stock up your farm, then there is no alternative.

There's plenty of space in Scotland that is ideal for sheep. So why not get rid of all those rough Highlanders and put in some Cheviot sheep? They're woolly and they're meaty – and they won't complain about being moved from lands they've occupied for centuries, and dumped in bog and moorland.

The Clearances were an appalling act of barbarity against the Highlands. Many people were thrown off their lands and replaced by Cheviot sheep.

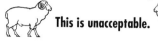 **This is unacceptable.**

Cheviot sheep are just not right for Scotland's rough lands. Replace them with Blackface sheep. These are much better suited for the environment of the Scottish Highlands and wet, windy and often cold weather. They will survive on even the poorest pasture.

What with Blackface sheep, overpopulation of deer (introduced by shooting estates) and the spread of rhododendron (introduced as a garden plant), by the end of the 20th century there will not be more than a few percent of native forest left in the whole of the Highlands.

Clear the Highlands of all wildlife, as well as people: buy a Blackface today

TV Guide

7.30 Dynasty

Last episode. The Stewart business has failed and despite last ditch efforts nothing can save it. James VIII dies in Rome, while his son Charlie does his best to raise some new capital. But it soon becomes clear that those he persuaded to join him will also be ruined. The House of Hanover is now in control and nothing can apparently save the Stewarts. Or can Charles leave his life of philandering and drinking, and retrieve the situation?

8.30 Who Wants To Be A Millionaire?

Just turn over Bonnie Prince Charlie to the government and they will send you the cash.

9.0 Groundforce

This week the team show crofters how to grow nutritious crops on rocks, stones, and peat bog.

HOW We Met
by
Doctor Samuel Johnson *and* James Boswell

■ I was privileged to make the Doctor's acquaintance in a bookshop, Number 8 Russell Street, London. I had long admired the man but was full of trepidation when we spoke.

I told him: 'I come from Scotland, but I cannot help it.'

The great man put me at my ease at once with, 'That, I find, is what a great many of your countrymen cannot help.'

How charming he is. And such a wit. We laugh from morning to night. There was once, someone asked what the most important thing in life was and quick as a flash the Doctor said, 'f***ing Sir, and after f***ing, drinking' and we all fell about.

Then another time, this man said to the Doctor that drinking was great because it kept your mind off dreary things, and the Doctor said: 'Why yes sir – if he is sitting next to you!' How we laughed. I could spend every minute in his company.

by James Boswell

■ I cannot stand Scotch men and I particularly cannot stand them on the make. Mr Boswell has dogged my footsteps since he pounced on me in a bookshop some-where. He's never out of my hair. Lately he seems to be taking notes every time I open my mouth! Not to worry, I'll give him the slip – a trip round the Highlands and Islands of Scotland.

Peace and quiet for months on end. I'll go to the Hebrides if I have to. He'll never track me down there.

by Samuel Johnson (Doctor)

Create Your Own
Robert Adam House!

*Scots Wha Hae proudly presents the
cut-out-and-keep Robert Adam House.*

All You Need Is Scissors and Glue

Simply cut out the pieces,
stick them together with
glue, and there you have it
– an 'accurate' scale model
of a Robert Adam house
from the 18th century.

*Revisit the Elegance
of the Scottish
Enlightenment*

You'll love the detail of the
*Scots Wha Hae Robert Adam
House*. Astragaled
windows, lovingly
reproduced stonework,
even details like the
chimneys, railings and
servants' area. It's a family
heirloom you can enjoy
again and again.

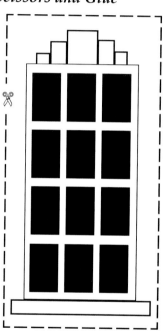

Collect All The Pieces

Scots Wha Hae is delighted to present the first part of
the *Robert Adam House* – the Ground Floor Drawing
Room Window. In future volumes, we'll present the
other windows, doors, even walls. Don't miss them!

Start your collection today!

More Lost Burns Poems Found

Controversial historian, Dr Ceilidh Minogue, has claimed that she has rediscovered several more fragments of Robert Burns poetry.

Robert Burns is Scotland's favourite poet and has many associations with Dumfries, not least that he died and is buried in the town. Burns wrote many of the most popular poems and songs in the world, including 'Auld Lang Syne', 'Tam o' Shanter' and 'Ae Fond Kiss'.

Dr Minogue was again in the Globe Inn in Dumfries when approached by a stranger, who gave her the verses in return for four double Aberlour malt whiskies and a packet of dry-roasted peanuts.

The verses, written out on slightly soiled toilet paper, are as follows:

To A Prostate

O' beastly muscle prostrate lobe,
Ye may hae had yer uses.
But now its fair to say:
Yer nothing but a nuisance.

Everyday we see ye,
The remains o' a TURP
Aye, yer the fash o' men –
Whae canny gang fir a pee!

The burning o' yer flesh
Och the smell pits us aff oor fuid
But then we hae tae think
It's doin' some man guid

A dribble no more, once yer in the jar,
A stream now flows, aye strong and far
Ha! Yer the bogle o' men around the globe
Wha ken o' yer presence when they're 60 year auld

Aye, it's true: a man's a man for a' that
And a prostate's a prostate – and that's a fact

Ae Winsome Wench

While I was bousin a' the
    nappie
My cronie Pete was unco
    happy
He'd been tae see a pantomime
And said he'd had a rare old
    time
But ane thing had him guy
    dumfoonert
So he came by tae talk aroon it
The panto dame, wi' ginger
    wig
And cutty sark, to dance a jig
Her skirts outlandish, all
    askew
And massive jugs, o' which
    she's tae
Plus bonnet, makeup and her
    bloomers
Nae knickers though (well,
    that's the rumour)
An' she seems an honest quean
Says Pete: 'What can this dame
    hae been?'
'Pete,' says I, 'It's quite a
    puzzle.
'The panto dame is in a
    muddle
'Though she's a he, with wig
    and lipstick,
'You never fa', quite, for his
    trick
'E'en in a dress, a wig, and hat
'A man's a man for a' that!'

Tam o' Shanter

First draft.

Droothy Tam was unco
    blootered,
When tae Aurk Kirk he
    drunken tootered.
He spied some soncie witches
    skirling.
The blether shite couldnae
    held frae purring:
'Weel done, Cutty Sark,' tae
    ane well-made wife.
Then he's full galloping on
    Meg for dear life,

Fleeing tae the Brig o' Doon,
    and gang sae fast,
For there the louping witches
    just cannae pass,
Last, at Meg's rump, Cutty
    Sark grasps but fails,
And that's the end o' Tam (and
    puir Meg's) tale.

That's Tam's tale on fleeing for
    his lifie,
That's the puir excuse he tauld
    to his wifie,
He was ane skellum shite and
    couldnae help it,
But Lord above his ears were
    skelpit.

Dr Minogue was today
unavailable for comment.

Scots Wha Hae!
Recipe for **Haggis**

Many people wonder what goes into that tasty and most Scottish of food, 'great chieftain o' the pudding race', the legendary haggis. No, it is not a creature which runs around hills, rather it is a delicious concoction of meat and spices to whet any appetite.

Lamb or mutton*, beef-suet, coarse oatmeal, onions, spices, salt, pepper, stock or gravy, [fillet of a fenny snake, eye of newt and toe of frog, wool of bat and tongue of dog, adder's fork and blind-worm's sting, lizard's leg and howlet's wing, scale of dragon, tooth of wolf, witch's mummy, maw and gulf of the ravin'd salt-sea shark, root of hemlock digg'd i' the dark, liver of blaspheming Jew, gall of goat and slips of yew sliver'd in the moon's eclipse, nose of Turk and Tartar's lips, finger of birth-strangled babe ditch-deliver'd by a drab, a tiger's chawdron, cooled with a baboon's blood]**

Traditionally, the mutton was actually the innards of the sheep, such as the lungs, liver and heart, and the whole mixture was put into a sheep's stomach.

*[]**These are optional: thanks to those three wifies recommended to us by Mr Banquo*

To make a vegetarian haggis replace all the meat products by pine nuts, small stones, shingle, metal pins, gritty lentils and wood chips.

You can even enjoy a haggis in most chip shops, deep fried in batter of course.

It's Enlightenment Challenge

We quiz the Scottish Enlighteners!

They're the cream of Scotland's thinkers and they've put Scotland on the intellectual map. Yes – it's the Scottish Enlighteners.

In Edinburgh's coffee houses and salons they seem to have all the answers. But let's turn the tables on the brainboxes – and see what they really know!

Ask Adam Smith about economics and he's in his element. His *Wealth of Nations* treatise on political economy caused a stir in 1776. But when we called up Adam and asked a few simple questions about money he wasn't so clever.

Adam's starter for ten was an easy one – how much is a pint of milk. 'What are you talking about?' asked the out-of-touch political economist. We repeated the question, but Smith was obviously flummoxed by the economics of the real world. He called us something unprintable and hung up the phone.

Following Smith in the hot seat was David Hume. This distinguished thinker has Edinburgh society hanging on his every word. But when we asked him an easy question about Emma Bunton (aka Baby Spice), he wasn't so forthcoming.

'Dammit sir, get out of my carriage,' thundered the eminent polymath.

Next up was the distinguished philosopher Thomas Reid. His works (*An Inquiry into the Human Mind on the Principles of Common Sense* (1764) and *Essays on the Intellectual Powers of Man* (1785)) have changed our view of the human mind.

But the Aberdeen-based scholar wasn't so smart when we asked him a few simple questions about popular culture.

'Which famous drag queen provided the voice of Grandma in Thunderbirds?'

'It's four in the morning,' croaked the man once described as David Hume's most significant contemporary. 'I'm sorry, but we have to take your first answer,' replied our interviewer. 'It was in fact Barry Humphries, now better known as Dame Edna Everage.'

So, there you have it. When they're really up against it, Scotland's smart-alecs aren't so clever. The emperors of the Enlightenment have no clothes.

Looking for an Extreme Adventure Holiday?

Take Your Life in Your Hands
Visit the
Highlands of Scotland

You'll marvel at the incredible scenery at the Ends of the Earth. Surely nothing civilised can survive in this rugged landscape!

See! The last untamed wilderness in the Empire!

See! The barbarity of the primitive inhabitants – they're barely human!

See! The unspeakable cannibal orgies of the Highland Scots!

BOOK NOW!
(Holiday insurance not available)
Ultime Thule Holidays Ltd, World's End, Edinburgh, Scotland

---

*The popular view of Scotland held by many even educated Europeans
was a country of savages; it was even seriously believed that the
Highlanders were cannibals.*

The Best of Times ...
Bobby Snatcher

Digging up a Few Old Friends

Those were the good old days. It was a grand life working for Edinburgh University. As I said to my mother, me who'd niver learnt to read, now I had a steady job with good pay along side all those professors and scholars.

I was on the night shift. It was quiet but it meant that you could get on with your job without anyone disturbing you. I worked mainly for the anatomy department and reported to Dr Robert Knox. I had my own lamp and a company shovel. But about a year ago I was let go. They'd got in a new firm of private contractors. When I asked why? – they just told me that the new company's products tended to be fresher. They were also able to supply on demand. Dr Knox said they'd had to move over to a 'just in time' method of supply. At least they let me keep the shovel.

I have to admit that I didn't really want to go back to the street cleaning but needs must. I'd moved back to Selkirk when the news reached me. The new company Burke & Hare Ptns (their slogan was *Dead on Time!*) got into trouble with the polis. I hear it all ended in acrimony. It just goes to show that not all these new management systems benefit the organisation.

Sometimes the old ways were just better.

Get the latest Super Soaraway
PARISH RECORDS
All the local news
• Who's doing what – to whom
• Births! Deaths! Marriages! Houghmagandie!
• Who's on the creepie stool this week?
• Don't forget the Page Three Crone
Still only a tanner!

Scots Wha Hae
EXERCISE PLAN
by our Health Correspondent Dr Robert Knox

The GUTBUSTER

'I tried the Gutbuster, and not only were my guts busted, they were strewn around the place in front of a crowd of onlookers at Smithfield Elms, then thrown on a bonfire in front of me.'
William Wallace

'When I was preaching the thinking of the Reformation, it was all too easy to snack on unhealthy foods. I was on the road all the time and soon piled on the pounds. But thanks to Cardinal Beaton, I burned off those calories – literally!'
George Wishart

Or try the MQS-Plan
Guaranteed!
You'll lose pounds of unsightly fat!
(Also bone, skin and brain)

NOTE: Please seek permission from Elizabeth I before embarking on the MQS-Plan weight loss procedure

Shortbread and Tartan

I joined Queen Victoria and her Consort, Prince Albert, several days into their first trip to Scotland. It is in fact only the second time since the Union that a reigning monarch has visited Scotland. It is a real honour for all us Scots. I was able to overhear some of their conversations, which I now have great pleasure in reporting to all our readers.

'Well this is a jolly nice little country, what say you Albert?'

'Me dear, it is most delightful. I really do think we should patronise it a little more.'

'Some of the young men have very well-developed legs. Their kilts seem to show them off particularly well. Albert you have very fine legs! You could wear a kilt for me? You could wear it in the evening when we retire to bed.'

'I shall wear one tonight.'

At this stage they both giggled a lot and whispered to each other. I mentioned to one of the courtiers that they seemed very informal. He replied that their majesties were remarkably athletic and the fresh air always seemed to invigorate them. I wasn't really sure what he meant.

At this point, even though it was only nine o'clock in the evening, their majesties made their excuses then and retired to their room. I suppose it must have been the tiring journey.

The next day I was again allowed to join the Royal party. We started with the royal breakfast. They had been presented with a dish of porridge each. They had never had it before but seemed to enjoy it. The Queen made a lot of remarks about how invigorating it was. Then she made a remark about his caber and they both started to giggle again. Albert mentioned having a bit of a Highland fling.

'That would be very amusing, Albert, and we don't have to worry about shortbread do we!' laughed the Queen.

They seem to speak in code. I presume it must be the London fashion. I mentioned this to their aide and he asked if I had never wondered about their many children. Yet, what does a revitalising bowl of porridge have to do with the blessing of children?

As it was all over my head, I decided that it was best to stay off the subject. I can, however, report they intend to rent out a small cottage for a weekend break and will be looking at the Balmoral glen in Deeside.

We've Had Our Chips

'Disaster has struck.' 'It's a nightmare!' 'Emigration is the only answer.' 'I'm off: last one turn out the lights.' These are some of the more measured comments from experts, after the failure of the potato crop this year.

We spoke to a few of the tenant farmers:

'Frankly it's a bloody disaster. We've been hungry before but we'll starve this time. I've had enough of the Highlands. It's a miserable place. It's always raining. It's freezing cold in winter and it's not much better in the summer. Then adding to the bloody awfulness of the place are the midges.'

'I'm off too. I've had enough preaching to keep me going through the rest of eternity and I'm sick of eating heather. I'm going to Anchorage. Apparently, it's a wonderful place, beautiful sun-kissed beaches, oranges growing wild just waiting to be picked, and beautiful girls in skimpy shifts.'

We asked him if he was sure that he didn't want to go to somewhere like California, but he was adamant that Alaska was the place for him. We wish all these plucky immigrants well wherever they choose to go. But we hope they'll carry a little piece of Scotland in their hearts.

Letters

Sir

I must protest in the strongest terms about this fellow MacAdam and his new-fangled ideas. I understand that he proposes to cover our countryside with unsightly strips of tar in the mistaken belief that this is somehow an improvement. The objections of ugliness apart, I can see that it is just another scam for the tollbooth owners to fleece us yet of more money. As if it wasn't expensive enough anyway.

Yours

Mr Brunt

TV Guide   Pick of the Day

7.30 **Tomorrow's World Special**

Peter Snow and some blonde bint pull faces over yet more outlandish gadgets which will never actually reach the shops. This week:

• Alexander Graham Bell demonstrates his new invention the 'telephone' which enables people to talk to someone in the next room.

• Joseph Lister reports on the dramatic effect his use of antiseptic has had on his surgical cases.

• Alexander Fleming discusses a new medicine which he claims will cure practically everything, yet is made out of mould.

• Henry Faulds demonstrates his new fingerprinting technique with much messing about with powders. Meanwhile in a special report on patent law, Kirkpatrick Macmillan wonders if he should copyright his invention the 'bicycle', but Judith Hann tells him not to bother as it won't catch on. And on location, John Loudoun MacAdam demonstrates his new road surfacing technique, known as 'MacAdamtar'.

Letters

Dear Sir

What is all this talk about Jute? The last thing we the good folk of Dundee need is some smart alec conman turning the heads of weak-minded industrialists with the idea of an industry based on some foreign plant.

What benefits are going to come from this foolhardy idea? Is it going to bring in work? Will it be useful for anything? I think not. It's just going to be another flash in-the-pan fashion accessory for dunderheads.

Tam Brunt.

Water Way To Go!

Cupar residents were asking, 'Water they talking about?' yesterday after turning down proposals for a new piped-water system and throwing their local council out along with the plans.

The town council had proposed adopting a piped water system on the grounds of health, hygiene and convenience. However, the scheme was so costly that Cupar ratepayers ejected the entire council rather than foot the bill.

The need for modern water systems has become more pressing thanks to the outbreaks of cholera, typhus and typhoid in 1832, 1848 and 1855.

Larger cities have led the way, establishing sanitary departments and appointing medical officers to monitor public health.

James Burn Russell in Glasgow, Matthew Hay in Aberdeen and Henry Littlejohn in Edinburgh have shamed reluctant councils into acting.

Since Glasgow's great cholera epidemic in 1848-9, nearly 50 miles of sewers have been laid throughout the city, and across Scotland major progress has been made with public health – sometimes against strong public resistance.

Vaccinations have been introduced, cesspools and middens removed, closes whitewashed, and piped water schemes introduced.

Glasgow got its Loch Katrine works in 1859 and Aberdeen got the Cairnton scheme in 1866. Edinburgh still has no major waterworks, but plans are being considered for a scheme at Moorfoot.

Meanwhile, Cupar residents are asking, 'Water we going to do now?' after rejecting the new scheme

Letters

Sir

I understand that there are moves afoot to put more of the beleaguered tax payers money into educating the farmers and fisherman of our country. What on earth do they need to read and write for? It is only going to distract them from the real job of farming and fishing,

Brunt

SCOTLAND INVADED

Now it's the upwardly mobile!

Scotland is facing another invasion as superior forces overwhelm the country – and it's all the fault of Prince Albert and Queen Victoria.

His purchase of Balmoral estate in 1852 has led to a flood of wealthy incomers all eager to follow the royal couple's example. Many of the brewing families have established homes in Scotland, the 'beerage' joining the peerage. Basses at Cluanie, Guinnesses at Achnacarry and Inverness-shire, and a Whitbread in Assynt.

The invaders met with little resistance. Many Highland landowners, finding that breeding sheep on their estates was not very profitable, were glad to rent out land to wealthy southerners. Vast tracts of sheep grazing lands have been turned over to game birds and deer for seasonal shoots.

And it's not just the very wealthy who are moving in.

Thomas Cook's first 'Tartan Tours' date from 1846 and John Frame followed suit, bringing the middle classes to the Highlands and acting like they owned the place, tramping round the moors and mountains to the fury of gamekeepers and ghillies.

There have been calls for the formation of a body to repel these invaders and keep incomers out of Scotland.

The proposed organisation would be called the Scottish Tourist Board, or VisitSomewhereelse as they are now affectionately known.

Scottish Journeys

There was a time when folk round here were content with the horse and carriage. But these new trains have opened our eyes. On a Saturday the whole world is now our oyster. We can get a seat in the second class carriage and before you know it we're in the grand city of Perth. Rose, my wife, will be in the coffee shop in McEwans, while I'll check out Murray's Tools on the high street. You should see the things they've got: it fair turns a man's head. I've got the bairns one of these new Meccano sets and we spend a' the evening building one of yon giant cranes, while the Crazy Gang makes us rock with laughter on the wireless.

Calm Down and De-stress

Scotland has given many things to the world.

Here, specially designed to reduce stress, are a new range of games. To be played by anyone from 75 to 95. Have you found reading the newspaper too racy? Have you found your heart beating a little faster at the thought of netball on the television of a Saturday afternoon?

If so, then why don't you try one of these very dull sports. Each one will reduce you to a torpor, they'll slow the blood, and allow your brain to relax after a hard days thinking. Yes, you too can kiss excitement goodbye when you take up golf, bowls or curling.

Specially designed clothes in ill-fitting styles reduce the chance of anyone finding you attractive and thus spoiling a quiet day out with emotional upheaval.

Breaking News

Despite being designed to be as dull as ditchwater, the successful women's curling team at the Olympics in 2002 have shown that indeed these sports can be exciting. Oh dear, but there is still Premier League football: Kilmarnock against Dunfermline on a cold dreich day in January should put anyone but the hardiest soul into a coma for days.

From the fevered imaginings of Robert Louis Stevenson comes the dark side of the ursine soul!

Doctor Jekyll and Mister Hyde Collectible Bear

By day, this cuddly little fellow is a respected London Doctor, ever treading the upward path. By night, he's out trampling small children and butchering prostitutes. Now you can get two teddy bears for the price of one – with the *Doctor Jekyll and Mister Hyde Collectible Bear.*

Millions have thrilled to Stevenson's tale of the beast within Man's civilised soul – inspired by the dark side of the Scottish spirit he observed while growing up in Edinburgh.

Now you can experience that archetypal struggle on your own mantelpiece. Who can forget Mister Hyde's reign of terror, as seen in plays, films and television? Now Stevenson's classic character is immortalised in this cuddly, if slightly sinister, heirloom bear.

A two-faced bear who's bear-faced too!

Watch out Sindy: Mr Hyde is on the prowl and his knives are sharp!

ORDER FORM

Yes, please send me the Doctor Jekyll and Mister Hyde Collectible bear. I have an unhealthy interest in violence, particularly towards women, and am interested in meeting a real lady some day. Who doesn't have staples down the middle.

Name _____   Address _____

Join our mailing list! Please tick your hobbies:

- ☐ Antiques
- ☐ Fine wines
- ☐ Lurking around bushes
- ☐ Going through people's bins
- ☐ Kerb crawling
- ☐ Stealing things off washing lines
- ☐ Owning a lot of guns
- ☐ Reading dodgy 'True Crime' mags with photographic reconstructions of real crimes
- ☐ Brass rubbing
- ☐ Streaking
- ☐ Flashing

☐ Please tick here if you do **NOT** want your details passed on to a third party, for example the Vice Squad

Names Shame of Scottish Writers

There has been a long tradition of writers using a pseudonym when publishing their work. For some, their original name didn't seem to be as catchy in the marketing pieces, others wanted to retain anonymity so they would be able to continue living in their community and observing the daily life of their neighbours.

Scottish writers were particularly keen on this and often had more than one *nom de plume* before they settled on the name they become famous with.

James Leslie Mitchell, the Aberdeenshire author famous for *A Scots Quair*, finally settled on Lewis Grassic Gibbon.

However, before he stuck with his final choice there are a few articles where he was obviously still undecided. The simian idea plainly struck a chord with him. When we look back at his oeuvre we find such versions as Lewis Grassic Baboon, Lewis Grassic Lemur and Lewis Grassic Gorilla. There is even one short try out of Lewis Grassic Orang Utang on a note to his milk man.

Scotland's most famous author, Walter Scott, toyed with the idea of changing his name with a view to increasing sales of his books, and he did write anonymously. Quite blatantly he tried to appeal to other markets.

So still to be found in specialist second hand bookshops are such titles as *Ivanhoe* by Sir Walter English, *The Heart of Midlothian* by Sir Walter Prussian and possibly, in a rather misguided attempt to sell copies into the Mediterranean islands, *Kenilworth* by Sir Walter Malta.

Robert Louis Stevenson initially attempted to escape the shadow of his successful grandfather, a lighthouse engineer, by changing his name. His choices weren't good and he encountered a number of lawsuits following his first few adopted names.

It is little surprise though when you become aware that there is a single copy of *Treasure Island* in the British Library by Charles Chickens, a short print run of *Kidnapped* by John Onion and two articles about cheese by Johann Wolfgang Von Gouda.

Stevenson was a sickly man and the added burden of courtroom appearances persuaded him to give up the idea of a pen name to return to his original name.

Although in one last act of defiance, and this shows how his ambition had been worn down, he did change Lewis to the now familiar Louis.

Celebrity **AGONY** Column
The Problem Page of
Miss Jean Brodie

Write in for the *crème de la crème* of advice from
the agony aunt who's in her prime.

■ My wife confronted me point blank about
lipstick on my collar. I kept quiet. Was that the right
thing to do?

*'You did well not to answer the question put to
you. It is well, when in difficulties, to say never a
word, neither black nor white. Speech is silver but
silence is golden.'*

■ I don't like wearing seatbelts, but should I put
safety first?

*'Safety does not come first. Goodness, Truth and
Beauty come first.'*

■ My husband has asked me to try something
called 'tarmacking' with him. Do you think I should
give it a try?

*'For those who like that sort of thing, that is the sort
of thing they like.'*

■ I am worried about satisfying my girlfriend. What
do women want in bed?

'Six inches is perfectly adequate. More is vulgar.'

Kirk Hits Out At Talkies

The new talking pictures were denounced this week by the Kirk which condemned them as meaningless filth.

Representatives met in Glasgow to discuss the films – mainly American – which feature, among other depravities:

- **VIOLENT** shoot-outs by gangsters

- **SKIRTS** above the ankle

- **BLASPHEMIES**

- **STRANGE** accents

- **GODLESSNESS**

- **MEN** lighting cigarettes for women

- and worse.

The Very Very Rev. Mungo Brunt of Blairgowrie said: 'These so-called 'talkies' are more than dangerous. They provide role models for our youngsters. For centuries they have been dressing like their parents, going out to work as soon as they could walk, and grafting from cradle to grave.

'Now these fancy talking pictures are giving them ideas. People may say that there's nothing to worry about, for no-one can understand these American accents. And they may be right for now. But the youngsters will imitate what they see. Things like new fashions, slang, romance and even (choke) fun.

'I predict the end of traditional Scottish values.'

ADVERTISING FEATURE

The *No Mean City* Theme Holiday

Authentic Scottish Hospitality
Come for a holiday in Glasgow

Accommodation

You will share a single-end with nine other holiday makers, many sleeping on the floor. The deluxe package offers you a space in the authentically fragrant cavity bed, along with a drunken grandfather and two feverish babies. You'll enjoy minimal queuing in the mornings, as our luxury tenements boast a toilet on every landing. Many of them work!

Outings

Day trips include razor fights on Glasgow Green, a visit to a pawn shop, and an hour queuing for 'the buroo' at the Labour Exchange.

In the evening, put on your paraffin to enjoy the burling at the *Gaydom Palais de Dance*, relax with an illicit drink in a shebeen, or visit the kinema and wonder how many illegitimate children are being conceived in the darkness around you.

End the night the traditional way – with a rammy. Break every bottle and window in the place before the police arrive, argue with the conductress on the tram home, and get your bit of stuff pregnant against the wall of the close.

Discover the Real Glasgow

Join our super competition and enjoy FREE food and accommodation – win a fortnight in Barlinnie!

Celebrity **AGONY** Column

Dear Mr Baird

I'm worried about my children.

All they seem to do each evening is switch on the radiogram and listen to it all evening. They never seem to read any more.

When their father and I were children we would read all the time. How do you think I could wean them off this device?

Yours sincerely, Anxious

Dear Mrs Anxious

Buy a television.

Best wishes, J Logie Baird.

Scottish Journeys

It's a rare beauty this car. It's at the cutting edge of technology. Red hot off the production line from Haleswood. You'll not find such a car anywhere in Wick, but this one here in my front drive. But you've got to look after it. You've got to love it as if it was your wife. Well, I suppose just a little more since this needs seeing to every week and the wife has come to expect a bit attention just the once a month. But you have to grease the nipples and decoke it and all that, and give a good rub down so that's it ready on the Monday. Why, in this little gem I can get to Inverness in a day and a half.

You know I saw it on the television in the window of a shop in Aberdeen. A fierce price those boxes of pictures. Yon Prime Minister was looking at one in the car show in London. I said to Flora: that, there, is the car for us.

Rock and Roll Reaches Stonehaven

Turned back at gate ...

A new craze has been spreading across Scotland – the dance sensation that sprang into life in the USA. The vibrant youthful jive, that captivates all who hear its seductive rhythms, has been wooing fans from Troon to Tain.

We spoke to some mod young 'cats'.

'So what do you think of this new music, young fellow?'

'Aye, it's jolly good fun of a Friday night. We all go down to the Beach Ballroom to where they've booked Angus Ochil and his Pasty Faced Pals. They're richt good and they soon have a couple of us tapping our feet.'

But there is one spot in the country that will be having none of this frivolity. Stonehaven has shut the door and put an extra bolt on it.

When we asked them why, one of the councillors shouted through the keyhole that they weren't having any of it and could we leave them alone.

Letters

Dear Sir,

I would like to point out that Stonehaven is not the only place that will be having none of this cacophonic rock and roll. Here on the West Coast, we won't be having anything to do with it either. Actually, since we don't have anything to do with music anyway, you probably hadn't noticed that we banned 'rock and roll'.

But I'd just like to point out for the record that we are against it too.

Yours sincerely
Reverend Brunt

An Appeal

Scotland

Help put this formerly strong nation back on its feet.

Scotland was found starving to death on the pavement in the Maryhill area of Glasgow. Recently it had fallen on very difficult times, abused and misused, and had started swearing at Gaelic speakers and abusing asylum seekers. Alcohol problems, poverty, poor housing, smoking, teenage pregnancy, lack of opportunity and a diet of burgers and coke have all taken their toll.

This once proud nation boasted such household names as Macbeth, William Wallace, Mary Queen of Scots, Robert Burns, David Hume, Adam Smith, Robert Adam, Sir Walter Scott, Robert Louis Stevenson, Andrew Carnegie, Alexander Graham Bell, John Logie Baird, Shirley Manson. Now it is hard put to muster more than deep-fried Mars bars, fish and chips, heroin addiction, bigotry, racism, a Scottish player in the Old Firm.

Can you help put Scotland back on its feet?

This is a difficult task. Scotland has many psychological and emotional problems, not least a complicated history and a complete lack of identity. It is also known to be confused and deceitful. It likes to portray itself as a tartan-clad Highlander, resplendent in kilt, bagpipes and claymore, eating haggis and drinking malt whisky – even when it is lying naked, neglected and filthy in the gutter.

Can you help? By sparing a few minutes of your time every week, and a few pence of your money, you can save Scotland from itself.

Help put Scotland back on its feet.

Shock Discovery of Council Housing Tenants

They actually like it, says leaked report

Council officials were scratching their heads this week as it was revealed that many of the people in council housing are satisfied with the standards of their homes.

'For years we have thrown up council housing that was the worst in Europe,' our source told us. 'Even English standards were better. With cheap materials and inefficient ideas – razing housing in established communities and relocating people to new schemes, placing people in tower blocks that isolated them from their neighbours – council housing had a very bad name. I wouldn't live in it myself.'

Now a surprising revelation shows that many of the people in council housing, particularly older people, think they've never had it so good.

'I grew up in a single-end in the Gorbals,' said one 75-year-old. 'We were 11 of a family sleeping in one room. Now I've got my own wee bedroom, living room and even a kitchen. It's like I've won the pools.'

Another pensioner told us, 'Younger folk don't know what it was like. When I was a lad, we had one toilet on the landing shared by six different families. Now I've got one all to myself and there's even a bath! It's paradise.'

The Braw Wee Toothill Report

I remember the guid auld days when yon John Toothill did his report about selecting which industries should be supported to increase prosperity in Scotland. Aye, it was a sobering read. In the old days, we just used to emigrate. But now they're saying it will have a serious effect on the work force.

Time was then we didn't have anything fancy like this new-fangled Scottish Development Agency that they're talking of – we just used to get on with it.

We didnae mind back then. Government intervention? A Victorian Jute Baron would do for us.

Changed times indeed.

Sponsor a Fan

For a little as £50 a week you can help a fan of Scottish football keep their habit alive.

Take Darren. He's a typical fan from Aberdeen. Next month he'll be faced with expenses such as buying magazines, a season ticket, travelling, the highlights video, the training video, the new home and away kit, three fanzines, posters, shares in the club that plummet in value, all the newspapers that might report on the team, and a novelty alarm clock.

Can you help Darren and others like him?

Please send your credit card details to: Goblinshead

TV Guide   Pick of the Day

2.30 **Carry On Up the Trossachs**

More bawdy mischief as the Carry On team descend on Hattie Jacques' Highland guesthouse amid much tossing ... of cabers. Sid James and Barbara Windsor have a Highland fling, while Joan Sims puts the 'bag' into bagpipes as Sid's wife. Meanwhile a grumpy gamekeeper shoots Terry Scott in the Cheviots and Charlie Hawtrey gets frozen in Bolfracks.

Cast

Hattie MacJapes	HATTIE JACQUES
Sid Bunnet	SID JAMES
Barbara Cutty Sark	BARBARA WINDSOR
Joan Scones	JOAN SIMS
Charles Drouthy	CHARLES HAWTREY
Terry Scot	TERRY SCOTT

Shortage of Letters Hits Highlands and Islands

Reports are coming in from many parts of Scotland that there is a shortage of vowels, and even some consonants, in Gaelic-speaking areas. Particularly scarce are As, Es, Is, Os and Us, and Ds, Hs, and Ns. Extreme cases include Bunnahabain, on the picturesque isle of Islay, being abbreviated to B'b', while A'Ghaidhealtachd (The Highlands in Gaelic) is rendered as 'G'lt'c', Obar-Dheadhain (Aberdeen) as 'b'r-', Inbhir-Nis (Inverness) as 'b'r-'s and Dun Eideann (Edinburgh) simply as ''.

'We are producing as many of these letters as we can,' said a leading lexicography and letter-manufacturing firm. 'It's just that those damn Gaels are using them up quicker than we can produce them. Road signs, maps and personal names, not to mention books of poetry. We do have plenty of Ks and Vs though,' he added.

Meanwhile, Surly MacLean of Raasay, told us: 'This is ridiculous. Although some Gaelic words are longer than English, many are actually shorter We use combined vowels and consonants to achieve a greater range of sounds. This is just a cheap jibe.

'Anyway,' he added, 'how d d you get my tel ph n n mb r?'

M   w l , t   pr bl m s spr   d g.

NEWS OF THE (small) WORLD
Local Woman Wins Award

Bunty McSlapper, whose mother was married to a man my mother knew at school, who used to go out with that woman who fell pregnant – what was her name? – anyway, her cousin was in my class at the school and his mother was married twice, once to the man that nearly got married to my aunt and who was related to that boy I was at school with who had the ginger hair, and he got married to a woman from Macclesfield and went to live in London, has won the local shop window dressing competition.

Scottish Journeys

I'm a very busy man and I often have to go to London.
My time is money so it is important that I get where I'm
going. Fortunately, when I fly down to Luton for a
business meeting I can just nip into the Inverness airport
and sometimes I can get there in a day and half, it's
amazing this modern travel. I must admit that I'm not so
keen on the food but I've no problem with a little whisky
on the way back.

90

WHO'S THE TOP HOT SCOT?
YOU DECIDE!

Says our showbiz correspondent.
The battle's on between Sean and Ewan!

Join our super competition to decide who's the best, Sean or Ewan.

Arrange these 10 features of fanciability in what you feel to be the order of importance, best first.

A   Hitting your wife with an open hand

B   Playing golf

C   Being close to your parents

D   Having the same accent in every film*

E   Supporting the SNP

F   Actually living in Scotland*

G   Getting your tadger out in almost every film you've ever done

H   Not wearing a wig*

I   Being pals with Nicole Kidman

J   Having lots of great gadgets and an Aston Martin

* Trick questions

How To Be An MSP
George Brunt

Once you've been elected, the key thing is to find out where the parliament building is, then it's just a question of turning up and collecting the money. No, I don't think there is anything else to it.

It's a Fiddle, Not a Muddle, says McLeish

Scottish composer Finlay Torquil McLeish yesterday identified a 16th-century musical instrument as a form of fiddle. The dilapidated artefact turned up at a car boot sale in Thurso and was described as a muddle, owing to an ineffectual restoration attempt some years ago. McLeish, an expert on medieval musical instruments and invented just for the headline, ahem, identified the incomplete instrument as a fiddle, not a muddle.

Freak Weather Conditions Rock Edinburgh

'Same All Day Long,' say Shocked Locals

Stunned residents of Edinburgh yesterday reported that the weather had been consistent for an entire day. A zone of freak stable weather, apparently stretching from Leith to the City Bypass, persisted from dawn to dusk.

Office workers, wearing light summer suits with raincoats and scarves, and carrying sunblock and umbrellas, were seen staring at the unchanging skies in mounting disbelief. Confused shoppers on Princes Street darted in and out of shops whilst taking off and putting on heavy coats at random, despite the fact that there was no unpredictable weather to shelter from.

Older residents were particularly perturbed. One Dalmeny Street worthy said: 'I'm 85 and I've never seen anything like it. I've lived here for 40 years and there hasn't been a day that you haven't had at the very least sunshine, rain and wind all coming and going. I blame all these asylum seekers. They make good curries, though.'

Hugh Grant, star of the film Notting Hill, in which four seasons seem to pass in a single day, was yesterday unavailable for comment. His spokesperson said: 'Well, they didn't exactly base that scene on a typical Edinburgh day, but it wouldn't surprise me. I went there on a school trip once and it was like visiting the Genesis Planet from Star Trek.'

Advertisement

Want to Make a Mint?
Want to Quadruple Your Cash in a Few Short Years?

Why Not Build a Bridge?

Scotland is a land of islands, lochs and rivers. In many places a bridge, causeway or tunnel could be a vital lifeline for islanders or travellers, improving communications, tourism and the economy, especially if the local ferry is forced to close. In fact, a bridge is absolutely essential for the welfare of the Highlands and Islands and many other parts of the country. But who cares? We are just here to make some dosh.

Photo of a bridge. These used to be supplied free but now offer amazing money-making opportunities.

So why not build a bridge? Then charge what tolls you like.
Locals and travellers are going to have to pay it,
and there is no risk for you.

You will get full government backing, and the support
of the Judiciary and courts despite any flaws there
might be in the original legislation.

So build a bridge today and start raking in the cash. Nobody can
possibly doubt that it is excellent value for YOUR money.

Coming soon: Roads, Hospitals and Schools.   Issued by the Scottish Executive.

Family Discovered Living in Last Century

Social workers have discovered a Scottish family living in the 1930s, say council bosses.

The Broun family is said to live in a tenement flat in 'conditions of squalor which are almost unthinkable in the 21st century', according to one source.

It is thought that as many as six adults and four children occupy the small tenement flat. The children are alleged to sleep four to a bed. An elderly grandfather, although not a resident, also seems to spend all his time in the house, meaning three generations live on top of each other.

Tensions flare frequently. Concerned neighbours told our reporter they have heard the dependent pensioner called an 'auld skinflint', a 'fly auld cadger' and other terms of abuse. The frail old man – who claims to be a Boer War veteran – can be seen struggling to walk up the street, wearing a dark suit which has not been in fashion since 1930. Rumours of geriatric abuse are rife in the street, and the family's formidable matriarch forces the brow-beaten senior citizen to eat his meals off a newspaper spread on the kitchen table.

Further investigation reveals that the younger Broun children are frequently in trouble at school. It's thought that some of them may not have had their births registered. And several of them – twin boys and a toddler – seem not to have been given names at all, and are always seen to wear the same clothes. Signs of neglect are evident as they go about the streets unsupervised, with dirty faces, and sometimes with nothing else to eat but a 'jeely piece'.

Although five members of the family are bringing in a wage, the family can barely make ends meet. Rows over money are common. The adult daughters constantly remind each other about 'that five bob you owe me', and trips to the pawn shop are not uncommon. Despite the occasional trappings of modern life – the odd mobile phone, a television that seldom seems to work – the family appears to be teetering on the edge of a standard of living not seen since the Depression.

SHAME OF SCOTLAND'S BIGGEST SCROUNGERS

We can expose that the frugal lifestyle of the infamous Brouns is a SHAM.

The family's plight touched the hearts of the Scottish people when we published their story last week. Our reporters told how they lived in cramped conditions, with little money and three generations in the same house.

But behind the shabby lace curtains lies the truth – **the Brouns are Scotland's biggest CON ARTISTS.**

We can reveal that Scotland's most grasping family:

- **LIVE IT UP with chocolate biscuits and takeaway food**
- **RAKE IN benefits: paid for by decent, hard-working Scots like you**
- **POP OFF to their second home for weekend breaks**

While the head of the household leaves for work every morning, he's not heading for the shipyards, that's for sure. No-one is sure exactly what he does and where he goes. But with all those children to support, surely he can't be up to any good.

Posing as a man doing a survey, our reporter spoke to Mrs Broun in her spacious kitchen. She's clearly not having to watch her pennies. Dishing out cups of tea without a moment's thought, she spoke frankly about her tearaway family.

'The bairns have been in trouble again,' she told us shamelessly. 'They got caught chapping on Girnie Green's door and running away.'

Amazingly, she thinks child hooliganism is nothing to worry about.

'Ach, it's just laddie-like. That Girnie Green's aye been an old moaner.'

And despite her life of leisure, she's still not satisfied.

'I fancy a fish supper for the tea tonight,' whined the grasping lay-about. 'But bet you the rest of them'll want something from the chippie as well!'

'Would you like a chocolate biscuit?' she asked. No expense spared. Offering our reporter swanky custard creams, she went on, 'I'd love to go on holiday abroad, or maybe have a week in Arbroath, Dunoon or Largs. But it's difficult finding the time to get away.'

'And with 11 of a family, it's not easy making ends meet,' she moaned.

The facts tell a different story. With three children at school and one under five, she rakes in the cash with nothing to do all day except a bit of dusting. The yo-yo-knickered scrounger claims family credit, income support, and gets free school meals and free dental treatment.

And who's paying for that, readers? You and me, that's who. With a whopping £36.00 cash in hand every week, it's trips to the bingo and the pictures whenever she likes.

What the Brouns don't want YOU to know is that they have a second home! Their luxury bungalow in the Highlands is the perfect retreat for a weekend break. Surrounded by acres of grounds and dramatic scenery, they get away from it all. How they pay for it has never been made clear.

We tried to get some good quotes out of a neighbour by asking about the head of the family, a small balding man well known in the street as a loudmouth and a bully. One resident said, 'He's a wee man, you see, that's what it is. I can't stand wee men. Hitler was a wee man, wasn't he, and Genghis Khan. And Napoleon. They were all wee men.' Then she started a conversation with her dog, and our reporter made his excuses and left.

Jock Tamson Blamed by Unmarried Mothers

Scotland's very high level of teenage pregnancy was slammed today by the authorities.

'In this age of contraception, teenage girls should know better,' said a spokesperson. 'If sexual intercourse is to be indulged in, and we would never encourage this, a condom should always be used. These girls can doom both themselves and their baby to a life of hardship and disadvantage, as well as increasing the risk of catching STDs and AIDs.'

Other authorities have condemned the preaching and dictatorial approach of the authorities and blamed one man, Jock Tamson. 'We have been trying to track down this individual,' said a spokesperson for Child Support Agency. 'He has been particularly 'active' all over the country. One mother of four living in Coatbridge, just turned 20, told us they were all Jock Tamson's bairns. We are starting, though, to wonder if it is just one person as the same father has been cited in Dumfries, Newton Stewart, Stornoway, Kelty, Motherwell, Largs, Ullapool, Carnoustie, Alloa, Port Glasgow and Scalloway.'

Jock Tamson was today unavailable for comment, and has no entry in the phone directory for Edinburgh and the Lothians.

Experts Choose Top Scot

William Wallace has been voted the most influential Scot of the Millennium in a poll of 500 top academics. Wallace led the Scottish army to decisive victory against the army of Edward I in 1297. He lit the torch of Scottish nationalism, and his heroism led directly to the modern independent Scotland of the 21st Century.

In second place was Gail Porter.

They've Got Off Scott Free,
Says Sir Walter

Sir Walter Scott, the father of the historical novel, is demanding royalties from every other novelist in the world.

Speaking from his grave at Dryburgh Abbey yesterday, he announced: 'To all intents and purposes, I invented the novel in 1814 with my famous series of 'Waverley Novels', starting with – funnily enough – *Waverley*. It's only right that I should receive my share of the rewards. People have been writing historical novels for donkey's years now – but would that have happened if I hadn't had the idea? I don't think so, somehow! But do I even get a credit on the title page? No.'

Critics have pointed out that, as he wrote his early novels anonymously, he released the idea of the historical novel into the public domain. But Scott is adamant that he deserves a share of all income derived from novels published.

'It is acknowledged – though not widely enough, in my opinion – that my novels changed the face not just of literature in English, but European writing too. Look at Victor Hugo, Tolstoy, Mazzoni. And the North Americans – that Fenimore Cooper for a start.

'And don't get me started on the thieving Scots! They're the worst! Robert Louis Stevenson and John Buchan didn't waste much time! If I'd been a younger man, and not dead, I'd have had it out with them I can tell you!'

Scholars have pointed out to Scott that his contemporary James Hogg was pretty quick off the mark with his novels as well. He said: 'Ah, that's different because he was a drinking mate. I know there was a big fuss because he wrote that biography of me which didn't pull any punches. But I thought it was quite funny! Anyway it didn't make any difference to me, because I was dead.

'And then there's the spin-offs. I never got a penny from that *Rob Roy* film. I wrote the book – you can't tell me they didn't have a quick flick through my novel before they started on the screenplay. But they haven't even stickered it with "The Book of the Film" or anything.'

Scott's financial situation was unreliable even during his lifetime. Although his novels were wildly successful, he was declared bankrupt in 1826 and forced to reissue the novels in hastily edited popular editions to try and make some money. He downplayed this aspect:

'I'm just asking for what's legally mine. And it's not as if they can't afford it. If I can persuade the Copyright Protection Agency to recognise my rights, I'll be getting a cut of Stephen King and J. K. Rowling's royalties. That'll see me all right.

'And justice will be satisfied,' he added hurriedly.

Scottish Dads Slam DVD

Scottish Dads spoke out yesterday against the new DVD format.

DVD, or Digital Versatile Disk, is a high-resolution format which allows an entire movie to be stored on a disk the size of a CD.

The picture quality is notably higher than that of a VHS recording and allows special features, such as scene selection, optional commentary, and the addition of new or extended scenes.

A number of households received DVD players for Christmas, and Scottish Dads were unanimous in condemning the new format.

One commented, 'disnae look that good to me' while another observed that it was 'nae bloody use at a''. A third Scottish Dad dismissed the DVD player with the words, 'I didnae bother takin' it oot of its box.'

DVD players have fallen in price over the past year, with many now available for less than £100.

TV Guide   Pick of the Day

2.30 **Big Bruthur Update**
   Day 38 in the Big Bruthur House. William Wallace has used up all the hot water and the housemates are not pleased. Meanwhile Rob Roy is feeding the chickens, who the housemates have named Urien, Gwallo, Morcant and Rhydderch. Mary Queen of Scots is preparing lentil quiche in the kitchen, while David Hume and Flora Macdonald are tackling this week's task – building a scale model of Melrose Abbey out of cornflakes packets. Little do they know their prize is nothing but a showing of a Krankies video.

*This newspaper is starting a new series. We've come up with a catchy new title so here is the first correspondence from '**The does anyone know column**'*

Does anyone know where the word 'clan' comes from?

■ It's from the Gaelic. It had three meanings, children, descendants and the tribe. It means that the members of a clan all have common descendants. Much like a big family. Of course those descendants might be back in the mists of time. The members will probably share the same name, they'll have fond feelings for a particular part of the countryside and they'll all want to wear the same tartan. Of course, just because you have the same name doesn't mean you are also a member of that Clan.

CMacA

■ Further to CMacA's reply: it's because all the members have that 'Clan do' attitude.

RF

■ Very droll RF. Could I add that the structure was based around the chief who was father of his people. He was meant to be the leader in war and the arbitrator in law and take an unbiased position. And I'd like to remind Colin MacAlasdair, who for some bizarre reason has become our Clan leader, about that last bit, the unbiased section. So think on it when the decision comes to the allocation of space for the burger bar conc-essions at the next MacAlasdair Highland games!!

TMcA

■ It's good to find out that Tom MacAlasdair reads a newspaper. So he'll find out when he reads this that after the virulent food poisoning that affected our last gathering we'll be offering the Burger Bar concession to someone who washes their hands!

CMacA

■ I'd like to join in the debate. Although in the 19th century there were many attempts both to systematise and romanticise clan society, the essence of it is that being in a Clan isn't just a question of getting all the benefits it but pledging loyalty to the chief. And that means not giving him a dose of the trots. Even if you did offer him a 25p discount when you visited him in hospital.

AMacA

■ You stuck-up brown noser, Alasdair MacAlasdair. The food poisoning was nothing to do with me. I doubt if it was food poisoning. Colin looked shaky on his legs before he even got to my van. Everyone knows he enjoys a drink or ten!

TMacA

■ *This debate is now closed. Please, please do not send any further letters.*

Pretty In Pinks

At time of writing, it looks as if Fox Hunting with Hounds has been banned in Scotland by the new devolved parliament. Many people claim that this is the will of the Scottish people as expressed through its parliament.

We say it is completely undemocratic and totalitarian for MSPs to make laws which we do not like.

Foxes – as we country people know but townies are entirely ignorant – are small, dog-like carnivores with pointy ears and bushy tails, and are allied with Satan. They prey on lambs, chickens and other farm animals, and the vulpine fiends even devour innocent bunny-rabbits, which are the farmer's friends as all country people know.

Many believe that fox hunting with hounds is a barbaric activity pursued by blood-thirsty buffoons.

We believe that this ban is a violation of the rights of upstanding country people to occupy themselves with traditional pastimes.

If hunting is banned, thousands of people will lose their jobs in Rockall, Taransay, Ailsa Craig and the Summer Isles. This is our contention. Indeed, this will be as much of a disaster for Scotland's employment as the closure of the steel works at Ravenscraig, the car plant at Linwood, the Invergordon aluminium smelter, most of the Scottish coalfield, and the decimation of Scottish manufacturing – all rolled into one.

It would be a tragic day if groups of riders clad in pinks, tartan jackets and jodhpurs, drinking from a stirrup cup and murdering their diphthongs, were prevented from tearing about the countryside, smashing through hedges and crops, and hunting indigenous wildlife going about its normal business.

We say stand up for democracy and ban the pesky Scottish parliament today. In fact, ban anyone who disagrees with right-minded folk like us.

Foxes in Arms About Ban

Today, we ask 'Reynard', a spokesman for foxes, what his vulpine brothers thought of the ban on fox hunting with hounds.
'Generally we are against the ban. Frankly, it is a pretty useless way to kill foxes, and we are equal to the challenge. Did you know that only 6% of foxes killed are killed by hunts? More of us are killed on the roads.'

Do foxes deserve to be treated as pests?
'You know, we are carnivores. We eat meat. It is true that once in a chicken shed we can go a bit mad, get caught up in bloodlust. But we do eat rabbits, mice and even rats – that must be good for farmers.'

Was he happy for the hunts to continue?
'Generally, yes. Although we do feel that the hunt is a bit one-sided. I mean we are solitary creatures and not very big, smaller than one of the hounds from the pack chasing us. We are armed with nothing more lethal than sharp teeth and keen wits. There must be 30 or 40 hounds and God alone knows how many horsemen. Does that sound fair to you?'

We asked if he thought it was an issue of class?
'Of course it is. Could you imagine if people kept foxes as pets on a council estate in Possil, then got together at weekends and went out hunting hounds. Not just that, but then followed their pack of foxes on motorbikes, roaring about the city streets, doing all sorts of damage. Then the foxes would tear the hound bodily apart. Can you imagine that being allowed for so long that it became a traditional sport? Ooh, I don't think so. If fox-hunting was 'working class' it would have been banned decades ago.'

Was there anything that could be done to improve the situation?
'Well, we think we should be better armed. I am not looking for anything like tanks or heavy armour. But some landmines, assault rifles and body armour would even things up. Oh, and some Stinger missiles.'

Next week the SLO tells us why salmon continue to resist imprisonment in fish farms.

Bus Wars:
The Empire Strikes Back

Most of Scotland's bus users do not know that many famous astronauts and spaceship pilots began their careers driving buses in Scotland's capital.

'I remember those years fondly,' said Han Solo, now pilot of the Millennium Falcon. 'The dog-fights we used to have with those First Direct fellows.' Han used to drive an LRT 44 in Edinburgh between Balerno and Wallyford. 'The most difficult part was the stretch between Portobello and Musselburgh. I once had a tussle with an FD 66. We were going so fast that we actually arrived at Brunton Hall before we left Kings Road, some two miles away. Those X-wings had nothing on a squadron of empty 66s trying to get some fares.

'We did the Joppa Pans run in one parsec,' he added.

Meanwhile Ellen Ripley, once flight officer on the Nostromo, was one of Edinburgh's first female drivers.

'It was quite hard at the beginning being accepted,' she (or one of her clones) said. 'Many men are troubled by a woman who knows who she is and what she wants. My abiding memory is not good, though. That alien with acid blood or that huge queen alien had nothing on a late-night run down Lothian Road on a Friday or Saturday night.'

Ripley did get a reputation for dealing with unpleasant characters, however. 'It is true that one drunken yobbo was smoking on my bus. As we rounded the corner into Princes Street, I blew him out of the goddamn airlock, er, I mean escorted him off the bus.'

James T. Kirk, captain of the USS Enterprise, began his days on the 23 Service from Trinity to Morningside. 'Serving Edinburgh was different from exploring space: although you should have seen some of the monsters we had on our vehicle,' he joked. 'We were always concerned that the engine would not be able to take it. We did reach Warp factor 9.5 once, however: not bad for an internal combustion engine before Dilithium crystals.' When asked why they had gone so fast, Kirk's chubby cheeks broke into a smile: 'It was five minutes past the end of my shift.'

BUS TIMETABLE	
Leith Walk, Edinburgh	
22	The Gyle
22	The Gyle
22	The Gyle
22	The Gyle
14	If you're lucky
22	The Gyle
22	The Gyle
22	The Gyle
87	Need to get to work on time?
22	The Gyle
22	The Gyle
49	Hope you're not in a hurry

Masons on the Mound
MORE REVELATIONS!

EXCLUSIVE! by *Andy Doorstepper*

A new scandal has engulfed the Scottish parliament with the discovery of yet more masons on the Mound.

Self-employed mason Jim Gilchrist is revealed as the latest man brought in to perform work at the temporary parliament building on the Mound in Edinburgh. It is alleged that Gilchrist (56) has been employed to:

- **POINT some brickwork round the back**
- **REPAIR a crumbling windowsill, and even**
- **GROUT some tiles in a sleazy toilet used by MSPs.**

The chain-smoking Gilchrist then sent in his invoice – and added a hefty VAT charge which the profligate Parliament paid without question.

We tracked Gilchrist down and confronted him with our allegations of corruption. Under intense pressure from our questioning, the overweight father-of-three crumbled, and he told all in a shocking statement to our reporter.

'I've got nothing to hide,' he blustered. 'I have been a mason for nearly thirty years. It's nothing to be ashamed of.'

And he alleged that the 'Masons on the Mound' scandal at the Scottish parliament was just the tip of the iceberg.

'There are plenty of masons in Edinburgh,' declared Gilchrist. 'It's a big city with a lot of stone buildings.' And in a thinly veiled threat, he told our reporter: 'You'd probably be surprised how many of us there are.'

Then he got into a van – a shabby Honda model with 'wash me please' written in the grime on the side – and drove off.

METRO *'Get a'* Life

Letters Page

■ Easter's very early this year, isn't it?
A. N. Oldgranny, Morningside

■ I don't like this fiddly paper money. We should never of gave up the gold sovereigns. That's that Napoleon's fault. They needed the gold to fund the war and there was no eggs, and the soldiers at the front had all the bananas.
Mrs McMuckle, Leith Walk

■ Easter's not as early as it has been. I've known it earlier than this.
Mrs Scalade, Bruntsfield

■ Oh, look, there's a particularly fine brown and white collie dog. Do any of your readers know the owner?
Ms B. Simmons, Canonmills

■ I'm on the bus going up Leith Walk and wonder if any readers could lend me money to buy a Mars bar?
Mrs H. Graham, Duke Street

■ I'm sitting further up the bus from you, and from what I can see it's not Mars bars you need, it's some fruit and a bit of exercise.
Mr D. Cumberland, Trinity

■ Sometimes Easter's quite late. It was very late last year, I think.
Mrs Threave, Montgomery Street

■ Yeah, yeah, Easter's so late it's on Boxing Day. Now shut up and stop discussing it.
Someone trying to get to work on the 14, Leith Walk

■ Does anyone know the attention span of a ...
Mr A. Anderson, Goldfish Crescent

■ How dare Mr Cumberland suggest I need exercise!
In any case I am hypoglycaemic and require sugar at
regular intervals. It is a recognised medical condition.
Mrs H. Graham, Duke Street

■ Hypoglycaemic indeed! In my day there was no such
thing as hypoglycaemia. You just got hungry, and ate
something. If you were sensible you ate something just
before you got really hungry. But from the looks of you,
you don't know when to stop. We're nearly at the
Bridges, why don't you get off a few stops early and
walk the rest of the way to your work?
Mr D. Cumberland, Trinity

■ Does anyone know the attention span of a ...
Mr A. Anderson, Goldfish Crescent

■ This was all trees when I was a girl.
Mrs McMuckle, Leith Walk

■ Oh, look, there's a particularly fine-looking Latin
bloke with a ponytail. Could any of your readers tell
me if he has a brown-and-white collie?
Ms B. Simmons, Canonmills

■ Does anyone know the attention span of a ...
Mr A. Anderson, Goldfish Crescent

■ It's not my fault I am large. Everyone in my family is
big. It's glandular.
Mrs H. Graham, Duke Street

■ Pffffffffff!
Mr D. Cumberland, Trinity

■ Oi! Mr Cumberland! Stop reading my copy of Metro
while I'm holding it!
Ms H. Brown, Leith Links

Lost Wicker Man Scenes Unearthed

The cult film 'The Wicker Man', which was filmed in Dumfries and Galloway, has had yet more of its missing scenes restored, bringing the total running time of the latest version to 437 minutes.

The missing footage came to light during the renovation of an ice cream parlour in Kirkcudbright. Film cans were discovered at the bottom of the freezer, and on inspection were found to contain unedited negatives, filmed in 1972 but mislaid and never included in the film.

The new scenes include:

* Sergeant Howie haggling with the landlord of The Green Man over getting charged for an extra bit of toast
* Sergeant Howie complaining that the shower ran cold in the morning (includes dialogue incompatible with the 'one day' edit of the film)
* Ingrid Pitt as the nymphomaniac librarian, charging everyone for a look at 'Tom and Jerry' (this dialogue does not appear in Shaffer's screenplay)
* An extra song performed by the sinister locals hanging around the Summerisle Fish and Chip Shop (slogan: 'Frying Policemen Tonight')
* Ingrid Pitt's character explaining her Polish accent by telling Howie that her grandparents moved from Summerisle to Poland during the 19th century famine, but that she returned to Summerisle in her childhood
* Diane Cilento's schoolteacher character explaining her accent by telling Howie she grew up in Ireland
* Lindsay Kemp's landlord character explaining he grew up in Pakistan
* Sergeant Howie complaining that there was no colour TV or kettle in his room at The Green Man
* Sergeant Howie complaining that there were midges everywhere
* Sergeant Howie ringing the STB to demand that The Green Man is downgraded to one-star
• Sergeant Howie wonders how it is this article found its way into this book, as do two of the authors

The extended version is due for DVD release in December, with a commentary by the old lady in the library near the end of the film, and one of the snails from the restored 'Gently Johnny' sequence. Britt Ekland has provided a commentary which will be dubbed onto the DVD by jazz singer Annie Ross. Ingrid Pitt declined to be involved as she is writing her own version of the film. Following his success in *The Lord of the Rings*, Christopher Lee has taken time out from his new career as a Cher impersonator to dig up the M3 in search of more missing footage.

DVD Extra

Featurette: Ekland on Scotland

'The most dismal place in Creation... Gloom and misery oozed out of the furniture.' Britt Ekland gives her (low) opinion of the locations used in The Wicker Man, including Newton Stewart, Creetown, Burrowhead and Gatehouse of Fleet.

Additional Featurette

Scotland on Ekland: Rod Stewart comments on his marriage to Britt

English Parentage Shock

For many years Scots have questioned the parentage of the English. Many believe that they are the sons of a thousand fathers, or that they are proof that the Welsh had sexual relations with sheep. Culturally they have little to recommend, beyond Morris dancing, jellied eels and football hooliganism.

Now a shock new report has found that the English are not even a racial group.

It's true. Genetically an Englishman cannot be differentiated from a Frenchman or German, or even the Welsh or Irish.

That's one in the eye for all those who purport the superiority of the English race. Perhaps now we can stop having endless repeats of that damned 1966 World Cup or that 5-1 victory as it now appears our southern neighbours are really as German as they are English. Agincourt and Crecy and all that hatred for the French is really just self hate. And even that enmity for the Welsh is just a case of parent abuse.

It is good to know with our own Scottish genetic purity and traditional culture spanning thousands of years that the Scots are now, without doubt, superior to the Sassenach.

Breaking News

Oh dear! Following the shock report that genetically the English cannot be differentiated from other races, it now appears that lowland Scots cannot be told apart from the English. Their genetic makeup is just too similar. Woe is me! We are actually as (and I shudder to use the word) *English* as we are Scottish, at least in the lowlands. And it also turns out that all Scottish culture is either Highland in origin or has been made up in the last century. Woe is me! It looks like the Scots are too similar to the English to be told apart, except that *they* won the World Cup and we didn't. Jings and crivvens!!

Scottish Parliament in Lesbian Kiss Row

The nation's newest soap opera, the Scottish Parliament, is set to score a major blow to its rival in Westminster with a sizzling new storyline which will help it grab audiences. The flagging flagship show hopes to win the ratings war when it screens its first **LESBIAN KISS** between MSPs later this week.

In the shocking scene, viewers will see a senior minister deliver a report on the Scottish rail network, then turn and give a lingering kiss on the lips to a well-known, controversial SNP MSP.

The Scottish Executive is bracing itself for complaints when all 16 of the soap's viewers watch the controversial scene at the close of Wednesday's episode.

But yesterday they denied that it was just a cheap publicity stunt designed to prop up the ailing Parliament.

'This gay kiss is no gimmick,' insisted Scottish Executive Whitewash Chief and Nippy Sweetie, Mr Nicol McTickle. 'The Scottish Parliament is dedicated to representing people from all walks of life, and like it or not gay issues are a part of modern Scotland.'

The Parliament has resorted to an increasingly bizarre series of plot twists to boost its viewing figures, including:

- **ROWS** over MSPs awarding themselves fat salaries and longer holidays

- **FURY** over the spiralling costs of the new Parliament building

- the **TRAGIC** death of First Minister Donald 'Father of the Nation' Dewar

- a **PROBE** into the 'Officegate' scandal of Henry McLeish, which nobody understood but everyone agreed was 'a disgrace'.

Future plot lines are thought to include Jack McConnell's Nazi gold exposé, UFOs buzzing New St Andrews House, and the Loch Ness Monster attacking the Scottish Office building at the Quay.

Applications are Invited for the Post of

Saint (Non-Religious)

A permanent full-time post, vacant for some years

Down the ages Scotland has produced many strong
and dedicated men and women – St Ninian,
St Columba, St Mungo, St Cuthbert, St Serf,
St Triduana, St Keir Hardie – who were able to put the
good of others before themselves, and stand up for
what they believed.

In this cynical, pragmatic and sceptical time, we are
now looking for someone to fill the post of saint and
meet all the duties and challenges this brings. This is a
difficult job, and although belief in God or gods is no
longer necessary, you should:

- **campaign tirelessly for the oppressed**
- **help disadvantaged people, such as by banning
  warrant sales**
- **refuse to pay unfair taxes**
- **protest against poverty, injustice and the evil of
  nuclear weapons**
- **be prepared to go to prison for your beliefs**
- **make opponents squirm**
- **often look dapper in smart suits**
- **enjoy getting a tan from a sunbed, even if you do
  look a bit orange in colour at times**

In return you can expect very little except thanks, the
respect of the Scottish population, and several
imprisonments at the hands of the authorities. At least
crucifixion is now banned, although watch out if the
Conservatives ever get into power.

The Correct Way To Sing
Flower of Scotland

O Flower of Scotland!   When Will We See Your Likes Again

Lustily		*Patriotically*	

That Fought And Died For   Yer Wee Bit Hill and Glen

With gusto		*Forte*	

And Stood Against Him   Proud Edward's Army

Uncertainly		*Trailing awa*	*Al dente*

And Sent Him Homeward   Tae Think Again!

Troppo Forte		*Forte Benson and Hedges*	

The Super Scots Wha Hae
WEATHER PREDICTOR

97% Accuracy Guaranteed!

GLASGOW

Monday	Rainy
Tuesday	Showery
Wednesday	Monsoon
Thursday	Drizzle
Friday	Plout
Saturday	Downpour
Sunday	Patchy sun

EDINBURGH

Monday	Rain, sun, some wind
Tuesday	Rain, wind, some sun, muggy at times
Wednesday	Sunny with rainy patches, some hail, and wind
Thursday	Windy with sunny patches and quite possibly snow
Friday	Rain, sleet, hail, wind, bright spots of T-shirt weather
Saturday	Bright and cold, turning to rain, warm later
Sunday	Changeable

Scots Win World Cup (Tickets)

The country had been racked with tension over the last few days.

All around Scotland there has been an air of expectation. Today was the big day, every one was on edge. What would happen? Some people couldn't bear the waiting and locked themselves away; others took to the streets shouting their confidence.

As the time approached, it was as if time had slowed the seconds felt like minutes, the minutes like hours. But at last

relief for the whole nation – two Scots had won tickets to the world cup in a lottery.

Despite having the World Cup tickets almost in their hands, the tickets then eluded their grasp and were blown away and disappeared down a gutter. 'We were so close to going to the World Cup,' said one anguished punter, 'but somehow managed to blow it along the way.'

'Oh well,' he added, 'there's always next time.'

Scotland Invaded:
But It's All a Mistake, Say Invaders

Aliens from Alpha Centauri, who invaded Scotland yesterday, have withdrawn their shock troops and confessed that they mistook the country for somewhere worth having.

'It's all been a terrible mistake,' said their leader, whose name is unpronounceable, yesterday. Speaking in the usual daft metallic voice he said, 'I had my eye on Canada – well, the other three eyes were watching 'The X Files' on TV – but we missed the turning at the Asteroid Belt Bypass and before we knew it, there we were in Cumnock. We had a look around but decided not to stay.'

The Alpha Centauri force joins a long line of invaders who claimed Scotland for their own but found their victory to be somewhat Pyrrhic. The Scots, the Romans, the Vikings and the Normans have all attempted to occupy the country in the past but generally decided not to move in.

Ten Great Scottish Things We'd Miss If They Weren't There.

1. The all-night bakery. The freshly made meat pie, still hot from the oven is fit for a king. Well maybe not Edward II, but definitely Edward VI.

2. Walking the hills in winter. The air raw, the sun is shining, water in the loch shimmers and you can see for miles across the landscape.

3. The Scottish pub. But only when it is full of people who are as drunk as you.

4. Whisky. A great drink and just what you need to give a pint of heavy that necessary spark.

5. The pipe band. They make you proud with their fancy kilts, all those lads with their cheeks puffed out. Then the rat-tat-tat of the drummers. They put the fear of God into the unwary and nervously disposed.

6. See You Jimmy Hats. A fine example of Scottish humour at its best. You can get musical ones as well!!

7. Hogmanay. 'Hug-me-now', suggests the Collins encyclopaedia. What a good idea for a party and best of all, two days holiday to recover from it.

8. Scottish Cuisine. Butteries, potato scones, haggis, Forfar bridies, Scotch pies, porridge, Dundee cake, scones, pie and sauce, oatcakes, and Luca's icecream.

9. The Ceilidh. There's no better way to spend an evening than dancing and shouting, and of course you can still have a great time even if you don't know how to do the dances.

10. Irn Bru! The best cure for a hangover in the world bar none.

Ten Not-So-Great Scottish Things We Wouldn't Miss If They Weren't There.

1. Midges. They're a bloody pain in the underwear. Speaking of which, at number two ...

2. Harris Tweed underwear. Not commonly worn, but even the thought is enough to give you nightmares

3. Caravanners on their way to the Kyle of Lochalsh. Who do they think they are? If the parliament did one thing it would be to provide the rest of us with bazookas so we could clear the road in front of us.

4. The lack of daylight in winter. Sometimes it seems like the sun never rises at all, especially the further north you are. Do we look like moles?

5. See You Jimmy Hats. A typical example of the paucity of Scottish humour. Do people really think that wearing one of these turns them into Oscar Wilde? You can get musical ones as well!!

6. Wet, cold, dismal summers. If you'd lost your calendar and landed in Scotland could you tell if it was winter or summer?

7. Golf. A sport to continually frustrate the honest man and bore the spectator.

8. Thistles. They may be our national emblem but they can make the wearing of a kilt a hazardous affair.

9. The M8 between Edinburgh and Glasgow. What a bloody awful road! It's usually raining when you drive on it. Is it just one giant roadwork?

10. The Scottish pub. When you are more drunk or more sober than everyone else, then it can be akin to hell on earth.

A Modest Showing
(based on a real conversation with a person from south of the Border)

'Of course I know there is part of England called Scotland, but I'm not sure where it is. Is it part of Yorkshire? To be honest, it is full of rough, rather stupid people. Have they got electricity up there yet? (ha ha ha). My friend went up there to do some shooting, and he said they were all so dim he couldn't understand a word they were saying. They just weren't bright enough to learn English. I suppose it is a bit of a shame that they're so backward. Is there a charity? We can give some money to help them.'

'Aye, you're right there: there isn't much we Scots have done. Well, I suppose the Romans never conquered us – they had to stop after they'd occupied England. But that's ancient history, isn't it? Then there was Bannockburn: probably the worst defeat an English army was ever to suffer. We've had our little successes but precious little to boast of, I know. A friend was telling me that, back in the 16th century, there were more universities in Aberdeen than in all of England. That makes me a little proud. Then James VI of Scotland actually become king of England as well: did you know the present Royal family are descended from him? But apart from that and the improvement of the steam engine, Tarmacadam, and penicillin, there's not much for us to boast of. Oh, and those artists, writers and poets: Burns, Scott, Stevenson, Adam, Raeburn, Ramsay, Buchan, Conan Doyle, Barrie. Well, there is always anaesthesia, television and the telephone, the threshing machine, radar and the pneumatic tyre, the fax machine, the decimal point and the Mackintosh coat. Then there was Glasgow Celtic being the first British team to win a European football trophy. Oh yes, and the Oxford Dictionary, the American navy, and the vacuum flask, malt whisky, the US National Park system, a cure for Malaria, and the novel. Then there is Thomas Telford and James Watt. And the fountain pen, fingerprinting and hypodermic syringe, the bicycle, antiseptics and rust paint, etc etc etc etc

114

Handy Guide to Britain

Many people outside Scotland appear to have difficulty identifying the difference between England and Britain. This was seen in spectacular style in identifying the winning British women's curling team as being from England, when in fact they were from Scotland. Incidentally, great win. Anyway, this handy guide should help those who are confused, and many who are not but are simply wrong.

BRITISH ISLES

All the islands of Britain, including Britain, Ireland and associated islands such as Shetland, Orkney, the Hebrides, Isle of Man, Anglesey, Isle of Wight, Scilly Isles and the Channel Isles. This is an encompassing term and is actually made up of two separate states: Britain; and Ireland, Eire or Southern Ireland.

BRITAIN (United Kingdom of Great Britain and Northern Ireland)

This is the biggest island of the British Isles, along with associated islands, except for the southern part of the island of Ireland (Eire or Southern Ireland) which is a separate country. The parliament for Britain is located at Westminster in London, England. Britain was created by a more-or-less equable union between England and Scotland. Scotland was never successfully invaded by England before the Union of the Crowns.

Consequently the present monarch is not Elizabeth II of Great Britain and Northern Ireland. The first queen of that name was only monarch of England. Scotland was a separate country at this time and had its own kings and queens, not least Mary, Queen of Scots. Indeed, on Elizabeth's death, it was James VI of Scots (Mary's son) who also became king of England (James I) in 1603. Anyway, Elizabeth is actually the first queen of that name to rule Britain.

Elizabeth is also not queen of England as England is not a separate entity when it comes to monarchs. Incidentally, Hadrian's Wall is all in England, and never formed any part of the border with Scotland.

SCOTLAND

This is the upper part of the main island of Britain, and includes Shetland, Orkney and the Western Isles or Hebrides. The border is roughly on a line between Berwick-upon-Tweed and Carlisle. Scotland makes up about one third of the total land mass, and has about one tenth of the population and makes all the good whisky. Scotland has a separate legal and education system from the rest of Britain, and a parliament in Edinburgh which controls most of the day-to-day running of the country (although not areas such as defence and most taxation, which are controlled from London). Scots also like to run Britain, but that bit is kept quiet as another great export from Scotland is politicians. Scotland has separate football and rugby teams, and competes as Scotland in the Commonwealth games. At the Olympics Scottish competitors contribute to the British Olympic Squad. It is safe to say, however, that most Scots dislike being called English.

ENGLAND, WALES AND IRELAND

This is the bottom half, as most Scots would agree, and can be simply defined as 'not Scotland'.

NEW! Expand Your Vocabulary
with Scottish Place Names

Airds Moss: Fluff found on a 13-year-old's upper lip

Ardler: Unpleasant disease of sheep

Balfarg Henge: Awkward walk caused by constricting underwear

Balloch: The feeling that the pile of ironing will never be done

Barpa Langass: Unfortunate intestinal complaint resulting in wind at both ends

Biggar: Old term of abuse (- off, - King, etc.)

Bute: Very scratchy wool, inappropriately used to make jumpers

Candida Casa: Well, put some yogurt on it

Corrievreckan: Feeling of giddiness experienced by hearing folk band

Crieff: Distress from visiting too many Woollen Mills

Crinan: Clothes made from man-made fibres, which discharge static electricity when rubbed vigorously

Dalbeattie: Very boring but bloody boxing bout

Dunbar: Night club which has fallen on hard times

Drumnadrochit: Exclamation of dismay on hearing the thumping bass of a car stereo

Dun an Sticar: Self-adhesive label (Gaelic); self-seal envelopes which have lost their gum (Scots)

Dun Troddan: Slightly sinister trail of brown footprints on pavement

Dun Telve: Any dark-coloured substance removed from an orifice

Dupplin: State of mind experienced by old biddies commenting that Easter is either late or early

Eilean Donan: To pee sitting down (if you're a man)

Eilean Molach: To pee standing up (if you're a woman)

Embo: Feeling akin to a slight stroke, experienced on Monday mornings

Girvan: Feeling of resentment from making too many charity contributions

Glasgow: Feeling of sudden anger provoked by a broken window

Gorbals: Particularly impressive bulge in a man's trousers

House of Dun: Cut-price megastore where the bargains turn out to be a rip off

House of the Binns: Collective term for a group of skips

Inchmahome: The ability to lock the door behind you after staggering home from the pub, despite the fact that you immediately pass out on the hall floor

Innerwick: Part of the auditory organ which expels earwax

Inveraray (pron. Invergargh): Exclamation made when tripping in Inverness

Jarlshof: Bit of hairy cheese found in back of fridge during desperate post-pub search for food

Kildalton: Pathological hatred of former James Bond actor

Largs: Dandruff (only in sideburns)

Linlithgow: Ancient charm to drive away demons (deriv. Lilith go, 11th C.)

Lochgilphead: Choking on a mouthful of frothy beer which then goes up the nose

Lossiemouth: Blue tinge on teeth caused by consumption of red wine

Lurgies: Illness caught from exposure to water from Montrose Basin

Monkland Canal: Part of the ear that blocks a nagging partner's comments

Maryculter: Young and otherwise inoffensive woman suffering from extreme road rage

Musselburgh: Party of overdeveloped but slightly camp body-builders

Muthill: Someone who leaves answerphone messages of such rambling complexity that the tape runs out

Neidpath Castle: Seldom visited tower house, requiring access road

Peebles: Kidney stones which prevent urinating

Peterculter: Young and otherwise inoffensive man suffering from extreme road rage

Portpatrick: Man who hangs around docks and accosts sailors

Prestonpans: Cut-price ironmongery which quickly loses its non-stick coating

Ring of Boggans: Stain of residue left in a lavatory bowl after a particularly messy evacuation

Ring of Brodgar: The morning after the curry before

Rothesay: The precise temperature of your bed on a Monday morning

Ruthwell Cross: Worse than Ruth Slightly Annoyed

Sanquhar: Heavy East-coast mist which catches in the chest

Scalloway: Skin ointment for eczema and contact dermatitis

Scrabster: Unpleasant skin condition with crusted blisters and pustules

Siccar Point: The precise moment you realise you are so drunk you will inevitably be seeing your drinks again

Solway Moss: Sign of an untended bikini line

Solway Firth: As Solway Moss, but the hair has extended up the abdomen

Strathpeffer: To season lightly (of food)

Strathspey: To over season (of food)

Tomnaverie Circle: Mark left around midriff by elastic of too-tight pants

Torphins: Bony upper arms of a stick-thin model

Uddingston: 17th-century emetic; 20th-century purgative

Yonder Bognie: Generic term for welcoming sight of nearby toilet when one is touching cloth

Yester: Manager who appears to agree with colleagues while secretly disregarding their views

NEW! COMPETITION
The Braveheart Quiz of REAL Scottishness

Take this short test: HOW SCOTTISH ARE YOU?

Being Scottish is not an accident of birth or a fact of geography – it's a state of mind. Wherever you live, you might actually be Scottish. Try this amazing quiz to find out!

1. On holiday in New York, which attraction do you look for first?

A   The Guggenheim

B   The Empire State Building

C   The chip shop

2. Your daughter gets married. Do you wear:

A   An exclusive dress, made specially by a high-profile young designer

B   An expensive off-the-peg Jenners outfit: she only gets married once

C   Your guid hounds-tooth coat that you bought in 1969: it'll see you out

3. A nightingale sings outside your window. Do you say:

A   Listen to that beautiful song

B   There's something you don't hear very often

C   Dinna make that noise, ma man's on night shift

4. Your house is on fire. Do you save:

A   Your photograph album

B   Your children

C   Your pair of wally dugs

5. Which of these valiant Scots do you most admire?

A   William Wallace

B   Robert the Bruce

C   Those lady curlers in the Winter Olympics

6. How do you judge someone's character?

A   By their postcode

B   By their car

C   By how often they take their turn at cleaning the stair

7. In your opinion, what should be the name for the Spirit of Scotland?

A   Scotia

B   Caledonia

C   Leanne

8. A neighbour's cherry tree is resplendent in white and pink blossom. Do you:

A   Tell them what a beautiful tree they have

B   Wish you had a similar tree

C   Tell them several times what a terrible mess it will make when all the blossom falls off and how long it will for take you to brush it all up

118

9. How do you view the new devolved parliament?

A   A waste of time

B   A waste of money

C   A waste of time and money, but at least some of your pals have cushy jobs and may even be MSPs one day

10. Have you considered the following as a fulfilling hobby?

A   Golf

B   Football

C   Deep-fat frying

11. What is Scotland's greatest gift to the world?

A   Penicillin

B   Anaesthetic

C   Sean Connery

12. Who is the most hated person of the 20th century?

A   Hitler

B   Stalin

C   Margaret Thatcher

13. Who is the most loved person of the 20th century?

A   Queen Mum

B   Michael Barrymore

C   Ewan McGregor

14. Why did you buy this book?

A   It was good value for money and there were some amusing articles

B   It was cheap and quite rude about the Scottish parliament

C   You didn't: you pinched it to light your fire

15. What do you consider to be Scotland's main industry?

A   Shipbuilding

B   Tourism

C   Skiving

16. How important is alcohol in Scottish life?

A   Important

B   Very important

C   What's an insurance firm got to do with your only interest in life?

17. How would you rate Scotland's chances of winning the next football championship?

A   Non-existent

B   Utterly non-existent

C   Non-existent, but you can never be quite sure as somebody has to win and we might just do it …

How did you do?

Mostly As:

You are not at all Scottish. You probably think a message is something you use to communicate with, rather than something you buy in a shop. Try living in a castle and walking about with a twisty walking stick.

Mostly Bs:

Good try, but no bottle of whisky. Try reminiscing about Robert Burns a bit more (without actually reading him) or daydreaming about winning the Lottery.

Mostly Cs:

Jings and crivvens: you could be turned into a float for Tartan Day and paraded down 6th Avenue in New York.

Famous Scottish Songs

Auld Lang Syne

Should old acquaintance be forgot,
And never brought to mind?
Should old acquaintance be forgot,
And auld lang syne!

Should old acquaintance be forgot? No, never! I am not going to forgive the neighbours from hell! Breaking branches off our fuscia! Just when it was looking so nice, too. Never a word of apology!

Then there was their damn cat, which pooed all over our lawn. Didn't matter what we did. Ugly cat with its lazy eye. I don't think poisoning it was going too far. Got what it deserved!

And their damned whirligig goes over our wall. His bloody crimplene trousers invade our air space when its windy. Perhaps we shouldn't have cut the legs off, but I can't tell you how furious we were.

And their damn ignorant offspring: their ball always ends up in our garden. They trample our flowers without as much as a 'can we get our ball back'. Shooting them with an air rifle showed them!

Ignorant swine! SWINE! ARRRRRGH!
Should old acquaintance be forgot,
And never brought to mind?
YOU MUST BE JOKING!